eating outdoors

RYLAND
PETERS
& SMALL

LONDON NEW YORK

eating outdoors

cooking and entertaining in the open air

Lindy Wildsmith

photography by Martin Brigdale

First published in the United Kingdom in 2006 by
Ryland Peters & Small
20–21 Jockey's Fields
London WC1R 4BW
www.rylandpeters.com

10 9 8 7 6 5 4 3 2

ISBN: 978 1 84597 131 1

A catalogue record for this book
is available from the British Library.

Printed and bound in China.

Senior Designer Steve Painter
Commissioning Editor
    Elsa Petersen-Schepelern
Editor Rachel Lawrence
Production Paul Harding
Art Director Anne-Marie Bulat
Publishing Director Alison Starling

Food Stylist Bridget Sargeson
Prop Stylist Helen Trent
Indexer Hilary Bird

Notes

• All spoon measurements are level, unless
otherwise stated.

• Eggs are medium, unless otherwise specified.
Uncooked or partially cooked eggs should not be
served to the very old, frail, young children,
pregnant women or those with compromised
immune systems.

• Ovens should be preheated to the specified
temperature. Recipes in this book were tested using
a regular oven. If using a fan-assisted oven, follow
the manufacturer's instructions for adjusting
temperatures.

Dedication

For all my family and friends who make eating
outdoors such fun.

contents

6   food tastes better

outdoors

9   barbecue know-how

10   perfect picnics

11   al fresco dining

12   barbecues

42   families outdoors

72   picnics

98   elegant al fresco

130   drinks

142   index

food tastes better outdoors

Once spring is in the air and we can feel the warmth of the sun, our thoughts drift back to the wonderful meals we have shared with family and friends in summers past. Enjoy a family meal in the early summer sun, cook a barbecue in the comforting shade of home, mix drinks at sunset, dine under the stars or picnic in the great outdoors and the memory will linger. Eating outdoors is about making the most of what nature has to offer and turning something ordinary into something extraordinary. Whether it is a simple snack or an elegant meal, food always tastes better outside. Make a Florida Refresher (page 132) and a stack of Scotch Pancakes (page 67) for breakfast and eat at leisure in the open air. The freshness of the morning and the sun on your face will instantly put you in a holiday mood.

Come the summer, the pull of the outdoors is irresistible. We all have a favourite picnic tryst, be it in a nearby park or garden, or far away in the countryside. Rather than making a mountain of rolls or sandwiches, try a Sicilian hooded sandwich, or *cabbucio*, filled with cheese, tomato and salami (page 78). Wrap it in foil and a cloth and off you go! Cooking outside is the ultimate in summer entertainment and a barbecue, whether it be in your own back yard or at a suitable local beauty spot, is fun for everyone. There are recipes for every taste, including Vegetable Kebabs with Bagna Cauda Dressing (page 40), Foil-wrapped Trout with Parma Ham, Olives and Mushrooms (page 39) and Aromatic Pork Burger in Pita Bread with Chilli Tomato Chutney (page 24).

Everyone loves their outside space. There may only be room for a tiny table, a couple of chairs and a flower pot or two, but it will be a special place where you can get away from it all. Plan a simple but elegant menu and luxuriate in the occasion. Outdoor food need not necessarily involve extra work, but it does help to plan ahead and to be organized so you can enjoy the occasion, too. The book therefore opens with practical hints and suggestions covering Barbecue Know-how (page 9), Perfect Picnics (page 10) and Al Fresco Dining (page 11).

Eating Outdoors is packed full of original and traditional recipes to inspire you into the kitchen and out into the fresh air. There are clear, concise instructions and many of the dishes can be prepared in advance. Small or large scale, a sandwich or a spread, there is nothing as pleasing as eating outdoors.

barbecue know-how

Getting the barbecue out is a sure sign of summer. Time to crack open a few beers, pull a cork or two and invite friends round. It does not have to be an elaborate affair – in fact, the simpler, the better. The smell of food cooking in the open air stimulates everyone's appetite and it is the kind of occasion when you can ask your guests to bring food and start the cooking when they arrive.

One of the dangers of a barbecue is finishing up with a mountain of charred meat all tasting the same. To avoid this, I have included recipes for colourful relishes and salsas, such as Mango, Kiwi and Coriander Salsa (page 15), delicious salads like Fennel and Orange Salad with Mint and Olives (page 16), and unusual barbecued vegetable recipes, like Sesame Sweet Potato Packets (page 20). There are mouthwatering recipes for seafood, meat and poultry – everything from Spiked Tiger Prawns with Lime and Chilli Marinade (page 36) to Nick's Barbecued Rare Roast Beef (page 31). For those who prefer to stay in the kitchen, the recipes contain instructions on cooking them indoors. The results are just as good and there is no fear of burning the food if your attention wanders to the guests and your glass of wine. For an extra flourish, the food can be put on the barbecue for a few minutes just before serving.

Choosing a barbecue

Most barbecues are charcoal or wood burners, although gas and electric ones are becoming increasingly popular. Traditional charcoal barbecues need time and patience to get going, whereas a gas barbecue is more or less instant. It does not give that traditional barbecue flavour, however, and requires a heavy gas cylinder.

You will also a few pieces of equipment, including long-handled cooking implements, such as tongs and metal spatulas, as well as tongs for the coals, a rake for the embers and a stiff wire brush for cleaning the grill rack. A small sharp knife is essential for cutting into meat and fish to see if it is thoroughly cooked. You may also need thick oven gloves. A preheated ridged grill pan set over the grill rack is ideal for cooking steaks, fish and vegetables as it seals the flavour inside and leaves attractive char-grilled stripes on the outside.

Lighting a charcoal barbecue

Choose a sheltered spot out of the wind and try to site the barbecue where the smoke will not waft over your guests or into the neighbouring property. Be considerate, not everyone loves the smell of the barbecue! Make sure you light the barbecue an hour before you want to eat to ensure you are cooking on embers not flames. So often the barbecue is at its best when there is no more food to cook. Break a few firelighters in half and mix them with a few pieces of charcoal, then put them in the middle of the barbecue. Pile on more charcoal to a depth of 5–10 cm and light. When the coals start to glow, spread them out to cover the base. When the flames have died down and there is no smoke, and the coals are glowing and covered with a powdery grey surface they are ready. This whole process will take 45–60 minutes.

Cooking on the barbecue

Once the coals are ready, arrange the meat on the grill and give it time to brown before turning. Once the meat has browned, turn it frequently and move it around the barbecue to ensure even cooking. You may need to raise the grill height if the cooking is too fast, or lower it so that it is nearer the coals if it is too slow. To lower the heat, dampen the coals slightly or close the air vent.

When using frozen meat or fish, ensure it is properly thawed before you start cooking. Make sure you cook chicken, burgers and sausages thoroughly. They should be piping hot all the way through, none of the meat should be pink and the juices should run clear. Cut into meats such as chicken to make sure they are cooked thoroughly. Cross contamination is one of the major causes of food poisoning, so it is essential to keep raw and cooked food apart.

Preparing the food

Get all the preparation done in advance – the day, the morning or an hour or two before you eat. Marinating times in the recipes are flexible, given as 1–24 hours so do what suits you. Salsas, relishes, dressings and salads can be made in advance, but green salads should be dressed at the last minute. Cover the food once prepared and refrigerate or store it in a cool place until you are ready to cook or serve it.

Safety tips
- Site the barbecue on level ground away from sheds, fences and trees.
- Consider wind direction before lighting as sparks can cause fires.
- Use firelighters or barbecue fuel; don't use petrol or paraffin to get the barbecue started.
- Keep a bucket of water or sand, or a garden hose nearby.
- Keep children, pets and garden games away from the barbecue.
- Leave the embers to cool completely before disposing of them.

perfect picnics

Picnics are a bit like Christmas, once you have organized everything you can switch off, relax and enjoy yourself and this is one of the reasons I love them. My picnics fall into two categories. The first is a simple spread, like those I remember from my childhood, of fresh seasonal produce, packed into boxes and bags. Everyone sits on a blanket on the ground and helps themselves, there are no plates, no cutlery and no fuss. Such a picnic is the ideal solution to a day on the beach or a foray into the countryside. Alternatively, they are grand occasions with shades of the British Raj, using tables, chairs, serving dishes, glasses, candles and flowers. These sort of picnics are perfect for a family get-together, a celebration, a special sporting event or an outdoor concert.

Putting a picnic together

Although it is fun to plan and organize a picnic, it can often be a spur of the moment thing and you don't always want to go to the trouble of making a lot of fancy food. A last minute trip to your local delicatessen to buy cold meats, canned and smoked fish, eggs, sausages, pies, pâtés and cheeses will solve the problem. Add fresh strawberries, cherries, tomatoes and cold drinks, and you have all you need. With a little extra time you can rustle up a filled loaf (pages 78–83) and make some dips (page 85) to serve with vegetables sticks. Try a single dish salad, such as Cherry Tomato Tabbouleh Salad with Pastrami (page 90), and bake a sweet treat (pages 93–97). For the really big occasion, try my Layered Salmon, Prawn and Potato Filo Pie (page 77) flavoured with tomato and basil. It will make a wonderful centrepiece and yet is easy to make.

Lastly, don't limit yourself to the picnic section of the book as there are delicious ideas and recipes for feasting outdoors throughout the book.

Children's picnics

Small children love to picnic on simple fare. Put raw vegetable sticks, cherry tomatoes, chicken legs, fruit and Triple Chocolate Chip Muffins (page 94) in a basket and send them out to the garden and see what fun they have. Pack up their backpacks with jam sandwiches or some freshly made scones (page 70) and take them on a walk or bike ride in the countryside and they will think they are in heaven. These are moments – believe it or not – they will remember to adulthood.

Packing your picnic

Transfer chilled food from the fridge to your cool bags just before you leave. Pack as much food as possible in plastic boxes to prevent it getting squashed. Put the boxes in first, followed by the frozen ice packs. Put anything that might get squashed on top. Pack warm food separately in a basket or hamper. Pack chilled drinks in a separate cool bag and if your picnic extends into the evening take a flask of coffee or tea and a little whisky or brandy to keep you warm.

Keeping food cold

When the weather is hot, it is essential to keep food and drink cool and to take plenty of water. Picnic hampers are beautiful, but do not keep food cold so use them to transport plates, cutlery, glasses and flasks and extras such as bread, nibbles and fruit that do not need to be chilled. Rather than buying a very large cool box, two smaller ones are often more practical. Freeze a couple of large bottles of water and pack them in the bottom of your bags to keep the picnic cold and provide extra cool water for later. At your destination, store the picnic in a cool, shady spot and keep the bags closed when not in use. On the beach, you can throw a wet towel over the cool bags to keep them cold.

Picnic essentials

- One large or two smaller cool bags with ice packs.
- Food, drink and water.
- Blanket/groundsheet or chairs and table.
- Hamper or basket to carry plates, cutlery and glasses.
- Bottle opener and corkscrew.
- Flasks of boiling water, plus what you need to make tea and coffee.
- Large bin liner to take rubbish home.

al fresco dining

We all long to recreate the wonder of eating outdoors on holiday, whether it be a long lunch in cool, leafy shade on a stifling hot day, a candlelit dinner in the balmy evening air, or a night spent chatting into the early hours. The weather may not always be as reliable at home, but when we are able to dine *al fresco*, it is a truly magical occasion.

Getting organized

As with all entertaining, it helps to be organized. When choosing a menu, think about what is in season and don't to be too rigid when shopping. If you are inviting new friends find out if they are vegetarian or have any food intolerances to ingredients such as wheat, seafood, nuts or dairy products. A vegetarian menu of Chilled Spinach, Rocket and Watercress Soup (page 103), Risotto with Sicilian Pesto (page 118) and Blueberry Frangipane Tart (page 126) would be eminently suitable and popular with non-vegetarians too. When choosing a menu for a special diet, cook it for everyone, otherwise you will just be making extra work for yourself. Once you have decided what you are going to cook, work out how much food you need – it's always better to make too much food so you don't run short. Make a shopping list and don't forget extras such as bread, chocolates, flowers, candles, nibbles, drinks and extra ice. You don't want to have to go back to the shops at the last minute.

Give yourself plenty of time to prepare and cook the food and don't choose complicated recipes you have not made before. Go for recipes that can be prepared or cooked in advance and baked or reheated when your guests arrive. It is your party and you should enjoy it too. Alternatively, if your *al fresco* meal is an impromptu tête-à-tête or a family treat at the end of a busy day you may prefer a last minute menu, such as Speck and Crayfish Cichetti Laced with Chilli (page 104), Instant Seafood Spaghetti (page 111), and Pineapple, Mango, Avocado and Banana with White Rum and Mint (page 125).

Drinks should be kept chilled until the last minute. If you are short of refrigerator space, put bottles and cans in a large receptacle in a shady spot and cover them with cold water and ice. If you are making a punch, such as Trafalgar Claret Cup (page 136) or John's Jug o'Pimms (page 139), have the fruit and ice ready in the freezer. Have some interesting non-alcoholic drinks too, like Melon and Ginger Refresher (page 135).

Setting the scene

Whether you have a large garden or a small paved area you can set the scene for a leisurely lunch or an elegant candlelit dinner. You don't even need special furniture as you can simply carry a table and chairs outside or throw a rug and cushions on the ground and dine Turkish style. You actually need very little to create a successful meal outdoors; you just need to seize the moment.

Set up your table in a sheltered spot out of the wind, preferably not too far from the house, as everything will have to be carried out and in again later. At lunchtime, provide some shade – a garden parasol is the obvious solution, but the natural shade of a tree or a plant covered trellis it is far more effective and also very pretty. Set the table with everything you will need, such as plates, cutlery, napkins, glasses and nibbles, and cover it with cloths until your guests arrive. If it is windy, make sure that any cloths are weighted down. On hot summer days we eat in the dappled shade of an old apple tree, and for birthdays we hang it with coloured streamers or twinkling lanterns by night with, and in late summer it is covered with its own picture book red apples.

Dressing for dinner

Coloured lights and pretty lanterns, and colourful plates, cutlery and glasses look wonderful on an outdoor dining table. Lay the table with a cloth and all the trappings you would use indoors, including flowers and lots of candles if dining after dark. You can also fill the garden with flares and lanterns and ponds with floating candles. Finally, warn your guests that they are dining outdoors so that they come dressed appropriately and be sensible if the weather turns cold and you are forced to abandon ship and go indoors.

barbecues

Just the mention of the word barbecue is enough to excite tired winter taste buds and to inspire the chef in everyone. The barbecue is a simple escape from the confines of the kitchen and the formality of eating round the table. Whether you serve a few choice sausages with a homemade relish or an exotic menu of grilled seafood, meat and vegetables, it's fun to cook on a fire and even more fun to eat freshly-cooked food out of doors.

mango, kiwi and coriander salsa

1 large ripe mango, peeled, stoned and cut into 1–2 cm cubes

4 kiwi fruit, peeled and cut into 1 cm cubes

finely grated zest and freshly squeezed juice of ½ unwaxed lemon

1 tablespoon extra virgin olive oil

1 tablespoon finely chopped fresh coriander

sea salt and freshly ground black pepper

serves 4

Put the mango and kiwi fruit in a glass bowl, then add the lemon zest and juice, olive oil and coriander. Season with salt and pepper to taste and mix well. Cover and refrigerate until required. Serve with grilled seafood, chicken or lamb.

peperonata

2 onions, thinly sliced

a large handful of fresh parsley, finely chopped, plus extra to serve

2 red peppers, deseeded and sliced

2 yellow peppers, deseeded and sliced

1 kg canned whole plum tomatoes, drained, deseeded and chopped

sea salt and freshly ground black pepper

olive oil, for frying

serves 8

Cover the base of a heavy-based frying pan with olive oil and put over medium heat. Add the onion and parsley and fry until the onion is softened, but not browned. Add the peppers, cook until soft, then add the tomatoes. Reduce the heat, cover and cook for 1 hour, stirring from time to time. Season with salt and pepper to taste.

Serve hot or cold, sprinkled with parsley, with grilled fish, seafood, poultry or meat.

parsley and anchovy relish

a large handful of fresh parsley

1 tablespoon salted capers, rinsed well and dried

6 anchovy fillets

grated zest of 1 unwaxed lemon

2 garlic cloves

4 tablespoons extra virgin olive oil

serves 4

Put the parsley, capers, anchovies, lemon zest and garlic on a chopping board and chop together with a large kitchen knife so that all the ingredients remain identifiable but tiny. Alternatively, put the ingredients in a food processor and chop finely, but take care not to reduce them to a mush.

Transfer to a bowl and stir in the olive oil. Cover and refrigerate until required. Serve with grilled meat or fish.

chilli tomato chutney

1 small piece of dried chilli, to taste

4 cm piece of fresh ginger, peeled and coarsely chopped

2 garlic cloves

2 shallots

125 ml white wine vinegar

1 kg canned whole plum tomatoes, drained, juice reserved, deseeded and chopped

200 g demerara sugar

makes 500 g

Put the chilli, ginger, garlic and shallots in a food processor and chop finely. Put the vinegar, tomatoes and sugar into a large, heavy saucepan, add the ginger mixture and stir well.

Put the saucepan over medium heat, bring slowly to the boil, then simmer over low heat for 1½ hours or until reduced by half, stirring from time to time. Should the chutney dry out too much, add a little of the reserved tomato juice. Let cool a little, then spoon into a sterilized jam jar and seal with a screw-top lid. Serve with grilled fish, seafood, poultry or meat.

When it comes to barbecues, or any summer meal for that matter, all you really need as an accompaniment is a big bowl of fresh salad leaves with a simple dressing and plenty of good, fresh crusty bread. However, there are certain salad ingredients, such as beetroot, fennel, peppers and tomatoes, that are so distinctive and delicious that they need singling out for special treatment. Here are three traditional Mediterranean recipes that do just that.

fennel and orange salad
with mint and olives

1 large fennel bulb, quartered and thinly sliced
2 large oranges, peeled, pith removed and cut into segments
a handful of fresh mint, finely chopped, plus extra sprigs to serve
2 tablespoons small red or black olives
3 tablespoons good-quality extra virgin olive oil
sea salt and freshly ground black pepper

serves 4

Put the fennel and orange in a large bowl, add the chopped mint, olives and olive oil, then season with salt and pepper to taste. Toss the salad well, turn out onto a serving platter and top with a few sprigs of mint. Cover and leave until required.

Note Do not be tempted to add any excess orange juice when you are mixing the salad as it will make it too watery.

beetroot salad
with coriander and olive oil

500 g small beetroots
3 tablespoons extra virgin olive oil
finely chopped zest of 1 unwaxed lemon
a handful of fresh coriander or parsley, finely chopped
½ teaspoon sugar
sea salt and freshly ground black pepper

serves 4

Trim the leaves off the beetroot, taking care to leave the base of the stalks attached. Boil the beetroot in a saucepan of simmering water for 30 minutes or until tender. Drain and leave until cool enough to handle, then peel and cut into slices.

Put the beetroot slices in a bowl, add the olive oil, lemon zest, coriander and sugar, then season with salt and pepper to taste and toss well. Cover and leave until required.

Note You may wish to wear gloves for peeling the beetroot to avoid staining your hands with the juices.

riviera salad

2 red peppers, deseeded, cut into thin rings and halved
3 large, firm tomatoes, thinly sliced and halved
a large handful of fresh parsley or mint, finely chopped
2 tablespoons good-quality extra virgin olive oil
sea salt and freshly ground black pepper

serves 4

Arrange alternate rows of the peppers and tomatoes on a serving plate. Sprinkle the parsley on top. Drizzle the olive oil all over the salad, and season with salt and pepper to taste. Cover and leave until required.

grilled aubergine
with tahini spread

freshly squeezed juice of 1 lemon

6 tablespoons light tahini paste

2 large aubergines, cut lengthways into 4 or 5 pieces

1 garlic clove, unpeeled and halved

1 tablespoon chopped fresh parsley

sea salt

extra virgin olive oil, for brushing and to serve

serves 4

Tahini is a tangy Middle Eastern spread made from roasted sesame seeds that is used to make dips, cakes and confectionery. It comes in two varieties – light tahini, made with hulled seeds, and dark tahini, made with unhulled seeds. The former is rounder in flavour and more suited to the aubergine taste. Tahini can be used as a spread or dip, or with other ingredients to make a dressing.

Put the lemon juice and tahini in a bowl and mix together.

Brush the aubergine slices with olive oil, then set over a preheated hot barbecue, or under a preheated hot grill, and brown on both sides.

Transfer the aubergine slices to a plate, rub with the garlic, sprinkle with salt and spread with the tahini mixture. Sprinkle with chopped parsley, drizzle with olive oil, then serve.

Variation You could use hoummus, basil pesto or olive pesto instead of the tahini paste and lemon juice.

4 red, yellow or orange peppers, halved lengthways and deseeded

4 tablespoons extra virgin olive oil

2 tablespoons balsamic vinegar

1 teaspoon coriander seeds, crushed

sea salt and freshly ground black pepper

to serve

a few sprigs of coriander or parsley, finely chopped

75 g feta cheese, crumbled (optional)

serves 4

grilled peppers
with balsamic and coriander dressing

Peppers are one of my favourite summer vegetables. Served raw in salads or as crudités, or roasted, grilled, fried or stewed, they add colour, texture and taste. My favourites are red ones, which are the sweetest, followed closely by the orange and yellow ones. The unripe green ones have a slightly bitter taste, but if you are a fan, use them too. Peppers grill beautifully and when peeled they have a rich velvety texture.

Put the pepper halves in a bowl, add the olive oil, vinegar, coriander seeds, salt and pepper and mix well. Cover until required.

Put the pepper halves, cut side up, on a preheated hot barbecue, reserving the excess dressing. Cook the pepper until the skin starts to blister and brown, and the flesh is tender. Alternatively, cook the pepper halves, skin side up, under a preheated hot grill. Scrape away the charred skin and discard. Transfer the pepper halves to a serving plate and spoon the reserved dressing over them. Sprinkle with coriander and serve with crumbled feta cheese, if liked.

Sweet potatoes are perfect for the barbecue because they cook quickly without pre-boiling. When tossed in dressing and wrapped in foil, the potatoes steam cook and absorb the flavours of the dressing. Care must be taken so that the potatoes do not burn through the foil where they are in direct contact with the heat. This recipe calls for individual packets, but one large packet does just as well. Cook them before the meat and put them on one side of the barbecue to keep warm.

sesame sweet potato packets

4 large sweet potatoes, about 600 g, peeled and cut
   into 4 or 5 slices
1–2 tablespoons vegetable oil
1–2 tablespoons shoyu or tamari soy sauce
1 tablespoon sesame seeds

to serve
1 tablespoon finely chopped fresh parsley

a barbecue with a lid

serves 4

Put the sweet potato in a bowl with the oil, soy sauce and sesame seeds and toss well. Divide between 4 large squares of aluminium foil, then crinkle the foil up around them and close tightly. Put the foil packets on a preheated hot barbecue, close the lid and leave to cook for 20–30 minutes or until tender. Alternatively, place the foil packets on a baking sheet and bake in a preheated oven at 180°C (350°F) Gas 4 for 20 minutes or until tender.

When ready to serve, open up the packets and sprinkle a little parsley on the sweet potatoes.

Note An even easier way to cook sesame sweet potatoes is to boil the potatoes for 4–5 minutes or until tender, then drain and put in a bowl. Add the soy sauce, sesame seeds and parsley and toss well.

grilled thai pork with stir-fried noodles

This versatile Thai-inspired marinade can be used to cook any meat or fish. Like many Thai recipes, it contains a lot of ingredients, but don't be put off. A top tip is to make a double quantity and refrigerate what you don't use in a sealed container for another occasion. As many of my marinades are inspired by Oriental flavours, I often serve barbecued meat and fish with noodles, but bread, rice or potatoes are equally delicious.

To make the marinade, put the ingredients in a food processor and reduce to a paste. Next, lay the slices of pork out in a single layer on a plate, then spoon over the marinade, turning the meat over so that the marinade is evenly distributed. Cover and leave for 1–24 hours to suit. (If marinating for more than 1 hour, put the pork in the refrigerator.)

When ready to cook, put the pork slices on a preheated hot barbecue, under a preheated hot grill or on a stove-top grill pan. Cook the pork for 20–30 minutes on each side or until browned. Cut into one of the slices to make sure it is cooked in the middle – if it is still pink, cook for an extra 10 minutes.

Bring a large saucepan of water to the boil and cook the noodles according to the instructions on the packet. Drain the noodles in a colander, reserving half of the cooking water and returning it to the saucepan. Set the colander containing the noodles over the saucepan.

Put the ginger, garlic and shallots in a food processor and chop finely. Heat the grapeseed oil in a wok or large pan, then add the ginger mixture and stir-fry over medium heat until soft. Add the carrot and leek and stir-fry until al dente.

Pour the reserved cooking water through the noodles to prevent them sticking together, drain lightly and add to the wok. Add the stock and toss well until the vegetables are well distributed among the noodles.

Transfer the noodles to a large serving platter and drizzle generously with sesame oil and soy sauce. Arrange the pork slices on top, drizzle a little more sesame oil on the meat and sprinkle with snipped chives. Serve immediately.

Variation Try serving chicken thighs this way.

500 g pork tenderloin, trimmed and cut into 1–2 cm diagonal slices

stir-fried noodles

250 g noodles

4 cm piece of fresh ginger, cut into 8 pieces

2 garlic cloves, halved

2 shallots, cut into 4 pieces

4 tablespoons grapeseed oil

150 g carrot, thinly sliced lengthways into matchsticks

100 g leek, thinly sliced lengthways into matchsticks

100 ml hot vegetable stock

marinade

1 small piece of dried chilli, to taste

2 cm piece fresh ginger, peeled

1 stick of lemon grass or grated zest of ½ unwaxed lemon

3 shallots

5 garlic cloves

1 anchovy fillet

1 tablespoon coriander seeds, crushed

1 teaspoon ground cumin

2 teaspoons cumin seeds

1 teaspoon ground turmeric

2 tablespoons shoyu or tamari soy sauce

1 tablespoon tamarind paste

1 tablespoon brown sugar

½ teaspoon sea salt

2 tablespoons olive oil

to serve

sesame oil

shoyu or tamari soy sauce

a small bunch of chives, snipped

serves 4

No barbecue – especially where children are involved – is complete without burgers, but burgers don't necessarily have to mean junk food. Not only is it healthier to make your own, but fun too as you can experiment with herbs and spices. This recipe can be varied to use beef, lamb or poultry, but make sure that you use good-quality meat. The addition of bread to the mixture gives a smoother texture and flavour.

aromatic pork burger in pita bread
with chilli tomato chutney

150 g bread
5 tablespoons milk
800 g minced pork
2 eggs
a handful of fresh parsley, finely chopped
4 garlic cloves, crushed
1 teaspoon ground cinnamon
a large pinch of ground cloves
1 teaspoon ground turmeric
a large pinch of chilli powder
the seeds of 4 cardamom pods, crushed
1 teaspoon sea salt
freshly ground black pepper
olive oil, for brushing

yoghurt dressing

300 ml natural set yoghurt
the seeds of 8 cardamom pods, crushed
a large pinch of sea salt

to serve

Chilli Tomato Chutney (page 15)
6 pita breads
150 g shredded iceberg lettuce

serves 4–6

To make the yoghurt dressing, put the yoghurt and cardomom seeds in a small bowl, add the salt and mix well. Cover and refrigerate until required.

Soak the bread in the milk for 10–15 minutes until soft, then squeeze the bread with your hands until it is almost dry and put in a bowl. Add the minced pork, eggs, parsley, garlic, spices, salt and plenty of pepper. Mix well, cover and leave to stand for 60 minutes.

Shape the meat mixture into 12 burgers. Cover and refrigerate until required.

When ready to cook, brush the burgers lightly with olive oil and cook them on a preheated hot barbecue for 20 minutes, turning them from time to time to avoid burning. Cut into one of the burgers to make sure it is cooked in the middle – if it is still pink, cook for an extra 5–10 minutes. Alternatively, cook the burgers in a frying pan over medium heat for 20 minutes, or put them in an oiled roasting tin and cook in a preheated oven at 180°C (350°F) Gas 4 for 20–30 minutes, turning from time to time. Transfer the burgers to a plate and spread each one with a spoonful of chilli tomato chutney.

Heat the pita breads on the barbecue or in the oven until just warm. Cut each one in half, open and fill with lettuce, yoghurt dressing and a burger, then serve.

japanese teriyaki-style spareribs

Like hot dogs and burgers, spareribs are a must on the barbecue, and although you can buy them in a choice of marinades, I much prefer to marinate them myself. Whether I plan to cook them in the oven or on the barbecue, I usually buy whole sheets of ribs. This way, I can marinate and cook them whole, then cut them into ribs before serving, which makes them really succulent.

To make the teriyaki marinade, put the soy sauce, sake, mirin and sugar in a saucepan, set over medium heat and simmer until the sugar dissolves. Set aside to cool. Put the sparerib sheets in a large freezer bag, add the marinade, seal tightly and leave to stand for 1–24 hours to suit, turning every now and again to allow for even distribution of the marinade. (If marinating for more than 1 hour, put the meat in the refrigerator.)

When ready to cook, drain the ribs, pouring the excess marinade into a small saucepan. Simmer the marinade over medium heat until reduced by half.

Wrap each sheet of spareribs in a double thickness of aluminium foil. Put the foil parcels on a preheated hot barbecue and cook for 15 minutes. Open the parcels, turn the meat and paint the ribs with the marinade, then close the parcels again. Repeat this 3 times or until the ribs are tender. This should take about 1 hour. To make sure the ribs are well cooked, cut into the thickest part of the meat in the centre of the rib sheet with a sharp knife. If the meat is still pink, wrap the ribs up again and put them back on the barbecue for an extra 10 minutes. Once cooked, unwrap the ribs, then put them directly on the barbecue and cook on both sides to give them that special barbecue taste. Alternatively, put the marinated ribs in a roasting tin with 100 ml of cold water and cook in a preheated oven at 180°C (350°F) Gas 4 for 60 minutes, turning once.

Transfer the rib sheets to a chopping board and cut up the ribs. Put them on a serving platter and pour the remaining marinade over them. Serve with stir-fried noodles or sweet potato packets and a green salad.

*Note Mirin is a sweet Japanese seasoning made from glutinous rice and is available in Asian stores and large supermarkets.

2 sheets of pork spareribs, about 1.5 kg

teriyaki marinade
200 ml tamari or shoyu soy sauce
200 ml Japanese sake or dry sherry
200 ml mirin* or sweet sherry
4 tablespoons granulated sugar
freshly ground black pepper

to serve
Stir-fried Noodles (page 23)
Sesame Sweet Potato Packets (page 20)
green salad

serves 4–6

When it comes to meat, Sicily is synonymous with lamb, especially in spring. I happened to be in Palermo one Easter Sunday and, curious to know how the locals spent the day, I was told that they went into the woods to cook a roast. On our way back from lunch in a nearby town later that day, we took the scenic route through the hairpin bends of the forest-clad mountains. We were amazed to find clusters of anorak-clad *Palermitani* scattered untidily through the eucalyptus forests, clustered around camp fires, with boxes, bottles and baskets littered everywhere and cars abandoned along the roadside. Smoke wafted in every direction and the air was heavy with the scent of roasting lamb.

sicilian-style lamb cutlets
with lemon and garlic marinade

1 kg lamb cutlets
6 garlic cloves, crushed
freshly squeezed juice of 2 lemons
5 tablespoons extra virgin olive oil
1 teaspoon dried oregano
1 bay leaf, torn
freshly ground black pepper

to serve
100 g wild rocket
coarse sea salt
lemon wedges

serves 4–6

Put the lamb cutlets in a freezer bag, then add the garlic, lemon juice, olive oil, oregano, bay leaf and plenty of black pepper. Seal tightly and leave to stand for 1–24 hours to suit, turning from time to time to allow for even distribution of the marinade. (If marinating for more than 1 hour, put the meat in the refrigerator.)

When ready to cook, drain the cutlets, reserving the marinade. Put the cutlets on a preheated hot barbecue, under a preheated grill or on a hot stove-top grill pan, and cook for 20–30 minutes or until golden brown, turning the meat from time to time and basting it with the marinade as you do so. To make sure the lamb is well cooked, cut into the thickest part of the meat with a sharp knife – if still pink, cook the cutlets for an extra 10 minutes. Alternatively, put the marinated cutlets in a roasting tin with 100 ml of cold water and cook in a preheated oven at 180°C (350°F) Gas 4 for 60 minutes, turning once. (Reserve the pan juices to pour over the lamb when serving.)

Spread the rocket over a serving dish, place the cutlets on top, sprinkle with salt and serve with lemon wedges.

Cooking on a barbecue is a skill that has to be learned through experience and roasting a whole joint does need practice to get it right. My friends Nick and Sandra barbecue their roast on a regular basis and Nick has developed the perfect method for cooking beef. It is dark, crusty and smoky on the outside while succulent red rare in the middle. Nick says it is essential to choose a large, thick piece of meat weighing a minimum of 2 kg, as smaller, flatter pieces dry out too much. The meat should be lean, but have plenty of fat around the outside, as this will keep it moist as it cooks and will ensure more flavour. It is essential to have a barbecue with a lid for roasting meat.

nick's barbecued rare roast beef

2 kg good-quality beef, such as topside or sirloin

a charcoal barbecue with a lid and a ventilator

serves 8

Prepare the charcoal as usual – briquettes are excellent for this recipe. When very hot, push the briquettes out to the side, leaving a circle of coals with a hole in the centre the size of your piece of meat. Line this crater with aluminium foil, creating a 'dish' underneath to catch the juices.

Place a wire grill over the coals, put the meat on top and cook for 50 minutes, turning every 10–15 minutes, until cooked evenly all over. To increase the heat, prop the lid of the barbecue open a little from time to time. Alternatively, put the beef in a roasting tin and cook in a preheated oven at 200ºC (400ºF) Gas 6 for 40 minutes. When cooked, rest the meat for 20 minutes before serving.

Note Take care when raising the lid of the barbecue, as the fat in the foil may ignite. Should this happen, simply replace the lid to extinguish the flame.

marinated herbed steak served panino style
with hoummus, tomato and basil

It is well worth buying your meat from a local butcher if you can – good butchers know their animals, their meat and their customers. Although asking for what you need might seem more daunting than simply picking it up in a supermarket, it is well worth the extra effort for the superior quality of meat. A decent strip of fat around the steak makes for good grilling and excellent flavour. Choose dark, red meat, lightly marbled and a moderate amount of fat along one side. Fat is essential for flavour and keeping the steak succulent – you don't have to eat it.

4 good-quality sirloin steaks, about 200 g each
1 large beef tomato, thinly sliced
1 tablespoon olive oil, plus extra for brushing
12 fresh basil leaves
4 panini or muffins
sea salt and freshly ground black pepper
170 g ready-made hoummus, to serve

marinade
4 tablespoons red wine
2 teaspoons balsamic vinegar
4 garlic cloves, crushed
a large handful of mixed fresh herbs, such as rosemary,
    sage, thyme or parsley
2 tablespoons extra virgin olive oil
1 teaspoon black peppercorns, crushed

serves 4

To make the marinade, put the wine, vinegar, garlic, herbs, olive oil and black pepper in a food processor and reduce to a paste. Put the steaks in a large freezer bag, then add the marinade and seal tightly. Leave to stand for 1–2 hours to suit, turning the bag from time to time.

When ready to cook, remove the steak from the marinade and leave to drain. Brush with a little olive oil and transfer to a preheated hot barbecue or a hot stove-top grill pan. Sear on both sides until well browned, 1–2 minutes on each side for rare meat. For medium or well-done, cook for a further 5–10 minutes, then leave to cool slightly.

Meanwhile, put the tomato slices on a plate, drizzle with the olive oil and season with salt and pepper. Sprinkle the basil leaves on top.

When cool enough to handle, cut the steak into slices. Cut the panini in half, and toast them on the barbecue or stove-top grill pan. Spread half of the panini halves with hoummus, put slices of steak on top and top with the tomato and basil. Sandwich with the remaining panini halves and serve immediately.

As a general rule, I avoid cooking chicken breast. Firstly, it does not have the flavour of dark meat and, secondly, because the meat is thick and dense, it can easily become dry and stringy. The answer is to beat the flesh to between half and a third of its original thickness, as it will then cook quickly and evenly, retaining its moisture. Chinese five-spice powder is one of my favourite spice blends. Containing fennel, cinnamon, cloves, star anise and black pepper, it is distinctive and aromatic, without being overpowering or spicy hot, and it lends itself to marinades of all kinds.

char-grilled chicken breast
with mixed leaves and balsamic dressing

4 fresh boneless chicken breasts, about 1 kg

marinade

2 teaspoons Chinese five-spice powder

1 teaspoon ground ginger

2 tablespoons balsamic vinegar

1 tablespoon extra virgin olive oil

1 teaspoon sea salt

freshly ground black pepper

balsamic dressing

4 tablespoons extra virgin olive oil

2 tablespoons balsamic vinegar

1 teaspoon mustard powder

1 tablespoon freshly squeezed lemon juice

2 teaspoons sugar

sea salt and freshly ground black pepper

to serve

150 g mixed salad leaves, such as rocket, watercress,
    lambs' lettuce, radicchio or baby spinach

Sesame Sweet Potato Packets (page 20)

a ridged stove-top grill pan

serves 4

Lay a piece of clingfilm on a chopping board, put a chicken breast in the middle and flatten it with the palms of your hands. Cover it with a second piece of clingfilm, beat it flat with a meat cleaver, then remove the clingfilm. Repeat with the remaining chicken breasts.

To make the marinade, put the five-spice powder, ginger, vinegar, olive oil and salt in a small bowl, season with black pepper and mix well. Spoon this over both sides of the chicken breasts, piling them on a plate as you go. Cover and leave to stand for 1–24 hours to suit. (If marinating for more than 1 hour, put the chicken in the refrigerator.)

To make the balsamic dressing, put the olive oil, vinegar, mustard powder, lemon juice and sugar in a jar, then add salt and pepper to taste, put the lid on and shake well.

When ready to cook, put the chicken on a preheated hot ridged stove-top grill pan on top of a preheated hot barbecue and cook on both sides until charred, about 10 minutes in total, lifting the corners from time to time to check that it is not burning. To make sure the chicken is cooked, cut into the thickest part with a sharp knife – if it is still pink, cook for a few more minutes.

Cover a large serving platter with the salad leaves. Arrange the cooked chicken breasts on top and drizzle the dressing over the chicken and the salad. Serve immediately with sesame sweet potato packets.

Like peaches and cream, seafood and chilli are meant for each other. The trick is to use just the right amount of chilli so that it brings out the flavour of the seafood without masking it. Whole chopped chillies are aromatic when used sparingly, unlike chilli powder, which tends to dominate a dish. Cooked in their shells, tiger prawns retain their flavour and require minimum preparation. They also look fantastic and make ideal finger food.

spiked tiger prawns
with lime and chilli marinade

To make the marinade, put the lime zest and juice, olive oil, chilli, mace and salt in a small bowl and leave to stand for 5–10 minutes.

Meanwhile, insert the pointed end of the skewer into the head end of a prawn and push it through the entire length and out the tail end so that the prawn is straight. Lay it on a large piece of aluminium foil, then repeat with the remaining prawns.

Rub the prawns with the marinade, wrap them up in the foil and leave to marinate for 1–2 hours.

When ready to cook, open the foil parcel, lay the skewered prawns on a preheated hot barbecue and cook for 5 minutes, turning once, until the prawns turn pink. To make sure they are cooked, insert a sharp knife into a prawn. If it is still raw, cook for a little longer. Alternatively, wrap the marinated prawns in a large, loose parcel of foil, put on a baking sheet and cook in a preheated oven at 220°C (425°F) Gas 7 for 5 minutes. Open the parcel and return the prawns to the oven, uncovered, for 5 minutes.

Cover a large serving dish with the salad leaves, dress with a little salt and pepper and drizzle with olive oil. Lay the prawn skewers across the salad and serve with mango, kiwi and coriander salsa.

12 raw tiger prawns, shell on

lime and chilli marinade
finely grated zest and freshly squeezed
   juice of 1 unwaxed lime
2 tablespoons extra virgin olive oil
1 medium fresh chilli, chopped
a large pinch of ground mace
sea salt

to serve
150 g mixed salad leaves, such as
   rocket, watercress, lambs' lettuce,
   radicchio or baby spinach
sea salt and freshly ground black pepper
extra virgin olive oil, for drizzling
Mango, Kiwi and Coriander Salsa
   (page 15)

12 wooden skewers, soaked overnight

serves 4

foil-wrapped trout
with parma ham, olives and mushrooms

This is a very simple recipe that can be adapted to cook many types of fish, such as sea bass, sea bream, mackerel and fillets of salmon. Very thin slices of bacon or pancetta can be used instead of Parma ham.

Clean the trout, leaving the head on. Take a piece of aluminium foil, large enough to enclose one of the fish, and grease with oil. Lay one of the fish diagonally across the middle. Put a sage leaf, a slice of Parma ham, salt and pepper inside the fish. Crinkle the foil up around the edge of the fish. Put a second sage leaf on top of the fish, then add a quarter of the mushroom slices, 3 olives and 1 tablespoon of wine. Drizzle with olive oil and lemon juice and season with salt and pepper.

Close the foil loosely around the fish, like a pasty, and transfer to a preheated hot barbecue. Cook for 10–15 minutes, then leave to rest for 5 minutes. Alternatively, put the foil parcels on a baking sheet and cook in a preheated oven at 220°C (425°F) Gas 7 for 15–20 minutes. Serve in the parcels with new potatoes and a tomato and basil salad.

4 medium-sized trout or 2 large trout
   fillets, 800 g–1 kg
8 fresh sage leaves or sprigs of thyme
4 slices of Parma ham or thinly
   sliced bacon
8 small mushrooms, thinly sliced
12 small green olives
4 tablespoons white wine
4 teaspoons olive oil, plus extra
   for greasing
freshly squeezed juice of 1 lemon
sea salt and freshly ground black pepper

to serve
new potatoes
tomato and basil salad

serves 4

This makes a wonderful vegetarian option for a barbecue, as well as a tasty side dish or a starter for all. Bagna cauda, literally meaning warm bath, is an important part of the traditional food of the Piedmont region of Italy and is traditionally served fondue-style with cooked or raw vegetables. Every mountain valley has its own version. The ingredients are cooked over a low flame, creating a velvety sauce that can be served as a dip or poured over the season's vegetables.

vegetables kebabs
with bagna cauda dressing

vegetable kebabs

1 corn-on-the-cob, cut into 8 pieces

1 red pepper, deseeded and cut into
    8 pieces

8 cup mushrooms

1 yellow pepper, deseeded and cut into
    8 pieces

4 small onions

sea salt and freshly ground black pepper

vegetable oil, for brushing

bagna cauda dressing

3 garlic cloves

50 g salted anchovy fillets, rinsed
    and dried

25 g butter

125 ml walnut or olive oil

4 metal skewers

serves 4

To make the dressing, grind the garlic and anchovies to a paste using a mortar and pestle. Put a small pan over very low heat and melt the butter. Add the garlic and anchovy paste and stir well until the paste dissolves in the butter. Add the walnut oil and simmer for 10 minutes, whisking the mixture continuously.

Thread a piece of corn onto a skewer, followed by a piece of red pepper, a mushroom, a piece of yellow pepper and an onion. Continue threading the vegetables, this time in reverse order, finishing with a piece of corn. Repeat with the remaining skewers and ingredients.

Brush the kebabs with vegetable oil and sprinkle with salt and pepper. Cook on a preheated hot barbecue or under a hot grill for 20–30 minutes until tender, turning from time to time. Transfer to plates, pour the dressing over the kebabs, then serve.

families outdoors

We all love to be outside because it offers a breathing space for everybody. Family life revolves around mealtimes; even more so out of doors as the fresh air makes everyone hungry. This chapter is full of recipes and ideas for breakfast, brunch, lunch, tea and supper. It features simple snacks, rich salad meals, sweet treats and satisfying pasta dishes and pies for adults and children alike to enjoy.

Bruschetta toppings are easy to make and very versatile. Many work well stirred into pasta or rice, or blended to make a dip. Here are two recipes that make a delicious starter or light lunch. The first is an update on the classic mozzarella, tomato and basil salad, which originally came from the island of Capri, off the coast of Italy. In the second recipe, I have simply crushed the beans so that they still have texture, but they can also be puréed to a hoummus-like consistency. Try experimenting with different combinations of pulses, herbs and spices.

bruschetta with baby mozzarella, cherry tomatoes and rocket

200 g baby mozzarellas, drained and halved

250 g cherry tomatoes, halved

4 tablespoons good-quality extra virgin olive oil, plus extra
    to serve

1 ciabatta loaf, left out overnight to dry out, if possible

1 large garlic clove, unpeeled and halved

50 g wild rocket

sea salt and freshly ground black pepper

balsamic vinegar, to serve

a ridged stove-top grill pan (optional)

serves 4

Put the mozzarella and tomatoes in a large bowl, add the olive oil, season with plenty of salt and pepper and mix well. Cover and leave to marinate for 1–2 hours.

When ready to serve, slice the bread open lengthways and toast both sides on a preheated ridged stove-top grill pan over medium–high heat. Alternatively, toast the bread under a preheated medium grill. Rub the toasted sides with the garlic and drizzle with olive oil. Toss the rocket with the mozzarella and tomato and spoon onto the toasted bread. Drizzle with balsamic vinegar and serve immediately.

bruschetta with crushed butter beans and lemon dressing

250 g dried butter beans, soaked overnight, or 440 g canned
    butter beans, drained

1 ciabatta loaf, left out overnight to dry out, if possible

1 large garlic clove, unpeeled and halved

lemon dressing

6 salted anchovy fillets, rinsed and dried

a large handful of fresh parsley

grated zest and freshly squeezed juice of 1 unwaxed lemon

4 tablespoons extra virgin olive oil

1 garlic clove

100 g pancetta or farm-cured bacon, finely chopped

100 ml dry white wine

freshly ground black pepper

to serve

extra virgin olive oil

finely chopped fresh parsley

a ridged stove-top grill pan (optional)

serves 4

If using dried beans, rinse and place in a large saucepan with plenty of water. Bring to the boil, then simmer for 30–60 minutes until tender – the cooking time will depend on the freshness of the beans so taste before draining.

To make the lemon dressing, put the anchovies, parsley and lemon zest on a chopping board and chop together finely. Put the olive oil and garlic in a small saucepan and cook over very low heat. When the garlic starts to colour, discard it, increase the heat to medium and add the pancetta and the anchovy mixture. Add some black pepper and fry for 3 minutes, stirring continuously. Add the lemon juice and wine and cook over low heat for 5 minutes, stirring from time to time. Add the beans and cook for a few more minutes, stirring. Crush the beans with a potato masher to break them up a little.

Slice the bread open lengthways and toast both sides on a preheated ridged stove-top grill pan over medium–high heat. Alternatively, toast the bread under a preheated medium grill. Cut the bread in half, then rub the toasted sides with the garlic and drizzle with olive oil. Spoon on the beans and sprinkle with olive oil and parsley. Serve immediately.

Although adding vinegar to the poaching water will help keep the white of the egg together, the only way to make a good poached egg is to use fresh free-range eggs from a local source, if possible. No other way of cooking an egg tests the quality and freshness quite so much. The richness of the yolk, the freshness of the asparagus and the subtle saltiness of the pancetta is a heavenly combination.

bruschetta with asparagus, pancetta and poached egg

1 bunch of asparagus, trimmed
 (8–12 spears)

20 g butter, melted

½ nutmeg, plus extra to serve

8 thin slices of pancetta, about 70 g

1 tablespoon vinegar

4 eggs

1 ciabatta loaf, left out overnight to
 dry out, if possible

1 large garlic clove, unpeeled
 and halved

extra virgin olive oil, to serve

a ridged stove-top grill pan (optional)

serves 4

Cook the asparagus in a saucepan of lightly salted boiling water until tender. Drain carefully, taking care not to break the tips. Transfer to a plate and pour the melted butter over the asparagus, reserving a little, then grate the nutmeg on top. Keep the plate warm.

Fry the pancetta in a dry non-stick frying pan until the slices start to crinkle and brown. Turn and brown on the other side.

Heat a shallow saucepan of water until the water is simmering and add the vinegar. Crack open the eggs, drop them one at a time into the water and cook according to taste, 1 minute for a soft poached egg. Lift the eggs out with a slotted spoon and transfer to a plate, carefully draining off any excess water as you do so.

Cut the ciabatta open lengthways and toast both sides on a preheated ridged stove-top grill pan over medium–high heat. Alternatively, toast the bread under a preheated medium grill. Cut each piece of ciabatta in half crossways, rub the toasted sides of the bread lightly with the garlic and drizzle with olive oil.

Put 2 slices of pancetta on each piece of ciabatta, lay the asparagus across the pancetta and place a poached egg on top. Spoon the remaining melted butter over the top and grate over a little extra nutmeg. Serve immediately.

The combination of chicken livers, mushrooms and bacon makes a delicious pâté that freezes well, so it's a good idea to make a double quantity and freeze what you don't use. Spoon the pâté into ramekins before freezing so that you have small portions ready to serve. If you prefer a smooth pâté, blend the ingredients in a food processor until smooth.

chicken liver, mushroom and bacon crostini

Put the porcini mushrooms and milk in a bowl and soak for the length of time detailed in the instructions on the packet. Squeeze the mushrooms to get rid of the excess liquid and transfer to a small saucepan. Add the chicken livers, cup mushrooms, bacon, butter, herbs and a good grinding of black pepper. Put the saucepan over medium heat and allow the butter to melt, then stir well and cover. Cook for 10 minutes, then transfer to a food processor and chop roughly. Taste and add salt, if necessary.

Cut the baguette into diagonal slices, 1–2 cm thick and spread with butter and a thick layer of the chicken liver mixture. Arrange on 2 baking sheets and drizzle with olive oil. Cook in a preheated oven at 220ºC (425ºF) Gas 7 for 10 minutes or until the bread is crisp. Serve immediately on platters decorated with bay leaves.

20 g dried porcini mushrooms
200 g chicken livers, rinsed and dried
180 g cup mushrooms, quartered
200 g bacon, preferably farm-cured, cut into
    4–5 pieces
200 g lightly salted butter, plus extra for spreading
1 bay leaf, plus extra to serve
1 tablespoon fresh thyme or ½ teaspoon dried thyme
2 baguettes, left out overnight to dry out, if possible
warmed milk, for soaking
sea salt (optional) and freshly ground black pepper
extra virgin olive oil, for drizzling

makes about 48

It is now possible to buy a good range of quality pulses in cans and they all lend themselves well to this recipe. Tangy sun-dried tomatoes work well with the richness of pulses and the best ones to use are sun-dried tomatoes preserved in oil or sun-blushed tomatoes. You can use dried ones, but you must soak them first or they will be hard and chewy.

chickpea and sun-dried tomato crostini

Mash the chickpeas well, add the parsley, sun-dried tomatoes and olive oil and mix well. Add salt and pepper to taste.

Cut the baguette into diagonal slices 1–2 cm thick, arrange on a baking sheet and bake in a preheated oven at 220°C (424°F) Gas 7 until really crisp and dry.

Rub the toasts with the garlic and sprinkle with salt. Pile the chickpea mixture on the toast, sprinkle with parsley and drizzle with olive oil. Serve immediately.

400 g canned chickpeas, drained
a handful of fresh parsley, chopped, plus extra to serve
6 sun-dried tomato halves preserved in oil, drained and
    finely chopped
1 tablespoon olive oil, plus extra to serve
1 baguette, left out overnight to dry out, if possible
2 garlic cloves, unpeeled and halved
sea salt and freshly ground black pepper

makes about 24

This Catalan salad is a refreshing change from the more usual *Salade Niçoise*. The serrano ham makes for an altogether more savoury dish and the formal arrangement of the ingredients on a platter, as opposed to being chopped up in a salad bowl, looks stunning. Aioli is a Catalan favourite and is also delicious served with raw or cooked vegetables.

catalan salad
with tuna and aioli

100 g French beans

2 baby romaine lettuces

100 g thinly sliced serrano ham

4 hard-boiled eggs, halved lengthways

200 g good-quality canned tuna, drained and broken into large chunks

8 large pitted green olives, halved

2 tablespoons extra virgin olive oil

2 tablespoons sherry or red wine vinegar

sea salt and freshly ground black pepper

aioli

4 garlic cloves, unpeeled

½ teaspoon salt

2 teaspoons freshly squeezed lemon juice

1 egg yolk

175 ml extra virgin olive oil

serves 4

To make the aioli, put the garlic cloves in a mortar and bash them lightly with a pestle, pulling away the skin as it frees itself. Add the salt and grind the garlic to a smooth paste. Transfer to a large, wide bowl, add the lemon juice and the egg yolk and whisk with a metal whisk. Continue whisking as you add the olive oil a few drops at a time; as the aioli starts to thicken, add the oil in a slow, steady stream. This should take about 5 minutes. If you prefer a lighter mayonnaise, whisk in 2 tablespoons of boiling water. Transfer to a serving bowl, cover and chill until required.

Cook the beans in salted boiling water for 7–10 minutes until al dente, then drain and plunge into iced water. Drain and dry. Cover a large platter with lettuce leaves, then fan the beans around the rim of the platter, sticking out from under the edge of the lettuce leaves. Twist the slices of serrano ham and arrange them on the lettuce leaves, then arrange the eggs, tuna and olive halves on top. Drizzle the olive oil and vinegar over the salad, then add salt and pepper. Serve with the aioli in a separate bowl.

Variation Use chicken breasts instead of tuna.

The combination of colours and textures in this salad is a knockout. It can be made with other pulses, but black beans work particularly well, as they highlight the colours of the other ingredients. Rather than cooking just enough pulses for your recipe, cook a whole packet and freeze what you don't use in small containers. The texture does not deteriorate and they are a useful salad ingredient to have on hand.

herbed black bean and avocado salad

150 g dried black turtle beans, soaked overnight or
 800 g canned black turtle beans, drained
400 g canned sweetcorn, drained
1 large red pepper, deseeded and diced
a handful of fresh parsley, finely chopped
a handful of mixed fresh herbs, such as basil, mint, dill
 or fennel fronds, finely chopped
3 tablespoons extra virgin olive oil
1 avocado
1 tablespoon freshly squeezed lemon juice
sea salt and freshly ground black pepper

serves 4

If using dried beans, rinse, then put in a large saucepan with plenty of water. Bring to the boil, then simmer for 30 minutes or until tender and drain.

Put the beans in a large salad bowl and add the sweetcorn, red pepper, herbs and olive oil. Stir well and cover until required.

When ready to serve, peel and stone the avocado, then cut into small cubes and put in a small bowl. Add the lemon juice, season with salt and pepper and mix well. Add the avocado to the bean salad and mix well. Taste and add more salt and pepper, if necessary, then serve.

Everybody loves potato salad and it is also a great way of using up excess cooked new potatoes. That said, the best potato salad is made while the potatoes are still warm. The flavour of the mayonnaise and other ingredients permeates the potato, giving a richer, rounder taste.

new potato, smoked turkey and chive salad

1.5 kg salad potatoes
200 g good-quality wafer-thin smoked turkey
250 ml mayonnaise
6 large green pitted olives, finely chopped
a handful of fresh chives or fennel fronds, finely
 snipped, plus extra to serve
chive flowers, to serve (optional)

serves 4

Put the potatoes in a large pan of salted water, then bring to the boil and simmer until tender. Drain and leave until cool enough to handle. Meanwhile, cut half of the turkey into slivers and put in a large bowl with the mayonnaise, olives and chives. Cut the potatoes in half, add to the bowl, then mix well and transfer to a serving platter.

Roll up the remaining slices of turkey and arrange them around the outside of the potatoes. Sprinkle with chives, decorate with chive flowers, if liked, and serve.

Pasta is a great standby meal – quick to cook and always a favourite with kids. Its versatile nature means that you can throw just about anything from the store cupboard or the refrigerator in with it, whether it be vegetables, meat or fish. All you need to do then is add some homemade tomato sauce or béchamel, mix it and bake it in the oven. That is exactly how this recipe came about – it went down so well that the only problem was recreating it.

pot luck summer pasta

2 tablespoons coarse sea salt

500 g penne or rigatoni

800 g canned plum tomatoes, drained and deseeded

6 garlic cloves, lightly crushed

1 teaspoon dried oregano or 1 small piece of chilli,
to taste

150 g cooked peas, sweetcorn or sliced mushrooms

370 g canned tuna in oil, half drained

100 g cooked ham or chicken, cut into slivers

1 tablespoon salted capers, rinsed, dried and chopped

150 g mozzarella cheese, diced

50 g salami, finely chopped (optional)

15 g crisp breadcrumbs*

extra virgin olive oil, for frying and drizzling

béchamel sauce

40 g butter

40 g flour

400 ml warmed milk

freshly grated nutmeg

sea salt

serves 4

Bring a 5-litre saucepan of water to the boil, add the salt and the pasta and cook over high heat until slightly less than al dente. Drain, reserving 2 tablespoons of the cooking water, and return to the saucepan.

Meanwhile, cover the base of a medium saucepan with olive oil. Put over high heat, and when the oil is searing hot, add the tomatoes. Cook for 1–2 minutes, taking care not to burn the tomatoes, but allowing them to caramelize a little. Reduce the heat and mash the tomatoes with a potato masher, then add the garlic and oregano. Stir well, cover and cook for a few minutes, then add the mushrooms, if using, cover and cook for 20 minutes. Stir in the tuna, capers, peas and ham and heat through.

To make the béchamel sauce, melt the butter in a small saucepan, and when it starts to bubble, add the flour and mix well. Cook over gentle heat for 1–2 minutes, then whisk in the milk and continue cooking until the sauce thickens. Add grated nutmeg and salt to taste.

Add the sauce to the pasta with the reserved water and mix until the pasta is well coated. Stir in the mozzarella and salami, if using. Transfer to a large, shallow buttered ovenproof dish and pour the béchamel sauce over the top. Sprinkle with the breadcrumbs. Drizzle with olive oil and bake in a preheated oven at 220°C (425°F) Gas 7 for 20–30 minutes until golden. Serve immediately.

*Note To make crisp breadcrumbs, cut the crusts off a large, slightly stale, white loaf and lay them on a large baking sheet. Bake in a preheated oven at 100°C (200ºF) Gas Low for about 1 hour until they have dried out completely and are crisp all the way through. Leave to cool, break into large pieces, then put in a food processor and reduce to fine crumbs. Store in an airtight tin lined with a freezer bag and use as required. To make soft breadcrumbs, cut the remaining bread into large chunks, put in a food processor and reduce to fine crumbs. Transfer to a freezer bag, then store in the freezer and use as required.

This simple recipe is ideal for family meals or any unexpected guests. Buy a good-quality Italian-made dried pasta from your local Italian delicatessen. Boil it in 10 litres of rapidly boiling water with a good handful of added salt. Follow the cooking time on the packet, tasting it 2 minutes before the suggested time is up.

penne with mascarpone, spinach and pancetta

150 g pancetta, diced
1 garlic clove, finely chopped
500 g penne
200 g mascarpone cheese
50 g Parmesan cheese, grated, plus extra to serve
200 g young spinach leaves, washed and dried
sea salt and freshly ground black pepper

serves 4

Heat a large frying pan over medium heat for a few minutes. Add the pancetta and garlic and cook until the fat runs and the pancetta is crispy and golden.

Bring a large saucepan of salted water to the boil, add the pasta and cook according to the instructions on the packet. Drain, reserving 4 tablespoons of the cooking water, and return to the saucepan.

Meanwhile, put the mascarpone in a small saucepan, add the reserved water and heat through gently. Add to the pasta with the Parmesan and a generous grinding of black pepper, and stir well.

Add the spinach and garlic and pancetta, including the fat from the frying pan, and stir well. Serve immediately with Parmesan.

Variation You can vary the vegetables – try rocket or lightly cooked leeks, peas, broad beans, French beans or carrots.

Pies such as these are family favourites in our house. Small pies are great to take on picnics. You can vary the fillings according to your family's likes and dislikes. Try using peas or French beans instead of mushrooms, turkey instead of chicken and fresh tomato sauce instead of the béchamel sauce.

chicken, ham and mushroom pies

If using a whole chicken, put it in a roasting tin and season with salt and pepper, then cook it in a preheated oven at 200°C (400°F) Gas 6 for 1 hour. Remove from the oven and leave to cool. Increase the oven temperature to 220°C (425°F) Gas 7.

When the chicken is cool enough to handle, transfer to a chopping board and reserve the roasting tin with the chicken juices for later use. Pull the skin off the chicken and discard. Pull the chicken meat off the bones, cut into bite-sized strips and transfer to the pie dish.

Set the roasting tin of chicken juices, or butter if using ready-cooked chicken, over medium heat. Add the mushrooms, salt and pepper and cook for 5 minutes or until the mushrooms are tender. Add the flour and stir well, add the warmed milk and continue to cook and stir until the sauce thickens. Add the slivers of ham and stir again. Divide the sauce among the pie dishes and leave to cool a little.

Roll out the puff pastry into a 30–34 cm square. Cut out 4 circles the same size as the pie dishes. Brush the rims of the pie dishes with cold water, then lay the pastry lids on top, pressing the pastry edges together firmly around the rim. Brush the pastry lids with water and make several small cuts in the middle of the pastry.

Put the pies on a baking sheet and bake in the centre of the oven, preheated to 220°C (425°F) Gas 7 if not previously used to cook the chicken, for 20–25 minutes. Serve with new potatoes tossed in butter and mint, your choice of vegetables and Dijon mustard, if liked.

Variation Instead of using cooked chicken and ham, stir 300 g raw cubed cod and 300 g salmon and 150 g cooked peeled prawns into the hot béchamel sauce.

one 1.5 kg whole chicken or 500 g
    freshly cooked chicken meat
50 g butter (optional)
175 g mushrooms, thinly sliced
4 tablespoons plain flour
400 ml full-cream milk, warmed
100 g cooked ham, cut into slivers
250 g ready-made puff pastry
sea salt and freshly ground black pepper

to serve

new potatoes tossed in butter and
    chopped fresh mint
cooked vegetables, such as green
    beans, carrots, courgettes or brocolli
Dijon mustard (optional)

*4 small pie dishes, about
12 cm diameter*

serves 4–6

This recipe is based on the French classic upside-down apple tart, *tarte des demoiselles Tatin*, and makes a great summer vegetarian lunch, supper dish or starter. I have used the classic Tatin pastry, but if you are in a hurry, use 250 g ready-made puff pastry, which makes an excellent substitute.

caramelized vegetable tarte tatin

100 g butter

1 large red pepper, deseeded and cut into 12 wedges

1 large yellow pepper, deseeded and cut into 12 wedges

1 large fennel bulb or 2 large onions, cut into 12 wedges

2 small aubergines or 2 trimmed leeks, sliced lengthways into 8 pieces and halved crossways

4 garlic cloves, crushed

1 teaspoon fresh thyme leaves

sea salt and freshly ground black pepper

pastry

250 g plain flour

a pinch of sea salt

150 g softened butter

10 g icing sugar

2 egg yolks

to serve

1 tablespoon fresh snipped chives or fennel fronds

tomato and rocket salad

a tarte tatin dish or a heavy-based flameproof ovenproof dish, 20–25 cm diameter

serves 4 as main course or 8 as starter

To make the pastry, put the flour, salt, butter, sifted icing sugar and egg yolks in a large bowl. Mix quickly with your hands to form a soft dough. Wrap in clingfilm and chill in the coldest part of the refrigerator for about 30 minutes.

Meanwhile, heat the tarte tatin dish over high heat, reduce the heat, then add the butter and heat until it has melted. Arrange the vegetable wedges like spokes on a wheel, alternating the peppers, fennel and aubergines, until the dish is full. Season with salt and pepper, and add the garlic and thyme leaves. Cook until tender and caramelized around the edges, jiggling the vegetables with a wooden spatula from time to time so that they cook evenly.

Roll out the pastry to a circle 1–2 cm thick to fit the pan snugly. Put it on top of the vegetables and press down firmly. Prick all over with a fork. Transfer to a preheated oven and bake at 200°C (400°F) Gas 6 for 20–30 minutes until golden.

Run a knife around the edge of the pastry to loosen it, then put a large ovenproof platter face down on the top of the pan. Holding the platter and pan together, invert quickly, giving it a good sharp shake as you do so, onto the plate. Set aside to rest so that the caramelized vegetable juices soak into the pastry.

When ready to serve, remove the tarte tatin dish, sprinkle with chives and serve warm with a tomato and rocket salad.

carpaccio of melon
with raspberry sauce

Raspberry purée makes the perfect accompaniment to many fruits. More tangy than strawberry, it has a distinctive flavour and the colour looks spectacular on the plate. This vesatile dish works equally well as a dessert or a starter. Alternatively, try adding smoked salmon for the perfect breakfast or brunch treat.

200 g raspberries
4 tablespoons icing sugar, plus extra to dust
1 cantaloupe or galia melon
freshly ground black pepper
4 sprigs of mint or sweet cicely, to serve

serves 4

Set aside 8 perfect raspberries and put the remaining raspberries in a food processor. Add the icing sugar. Transfer to a fine sieve set over a bowl, then push through with the back of a wooden spoon.

Cut the melon into 8 wedges, discard the seeds and cut off the skin. Slice the wedges into very thin slices and arrange on individual plates or a serving platter with the raspberries. Dust lightly with black pepper and icing sugar, then cover and chill.

When ready to serve, spoon the raspberry purée over the melon, creating a pattern of lines over the fruit and the plate. Decorate with sprigs of mint.

fruit platter
with spiced caramel

Tropical and summer fruits are so luscious that they need little or no help from the cook to improve them. However, there are simple ways to serve them that give them an edge. A spiced caramel enhances and enriches the flavour of the fruit and, drizzled on the fruit in lines or spots, makes for a stunning dish.

250 g thinly sliced melon, mango, kiwi fruit
    or pineapple, or halved peaches, apricots
    or strawberries
200 g granulated sugar
3 tablespoons water
1 teaspoon ground aniseed or cinnamon
sprigs of mint or sweet cicely, to serve

serves 4

Arrange the fruit on individual plates or a large platter. Put the sugar, water and aniseed in a small saucepan, place over high heat and boil without stirring until it starts to change colour and has a thick and syrupy appearance.

Spoon the caramel over the fruit in a fine stream or in spots, creating a pattern over the fruit and the plate. Top with mint sprigs, then serve, with any leftover spiced caramel in a separate jug.

fruit fool

500 g rhubarb, cut into 5 cm pieces, or
plums, halved and stoned
100–125 g caster sugar, to taste

custard
250 ml milk
1 vanilla pod
2 egg yolks
1 tablespoon caster sugar
2 teaspoons cornflour

to serve
100 ml single cream (optional)
fresh mint leaves (optional)

serves 4–6

Fruit fools are the epitome of English country summer food and are the perfect way to enjoy acidic fruit, such as rhubarb, blueberries, greengages, damsons, plums and blackberries. To save time, you can use single cream instead of custard – simply mix it into the cooked rhubarb before pouring into the glasses.

To make the custard, put the milk in a small saucepan with the vanilla pod and bring slowly to simmering point. Remove the vanilla pod, rinse, dry and put to one side. Whisk the egg yolks in a bowl with the sugar and cornflour and slowly add the warmed milk, whisking as you do so. Strain the mixture back into the saucepan and stir continuously over low heat with a wire whisk until the mixture thickens. Pour into a clean shallow bowl to cool.

Put the rhubarb in a saucepan. Add the sugar, to taste, cover and cook over low heat for 5 minutes or until tender. Transfer to a food processor and reduce to a smooth purée. When cool, transfer to a bowl and stir in the custard. Spoon into tumblers and chill until required.

When ready to serve, pour a thin layer of cream over the surface and top each one with a mint leaf, if liked.

Variation For breakfast, use natural set yoghurt instead of custard and serve topped with your favourite muesli.

There is no quicker nor more simple recipe for a tea-time or breakfast treat than Scotch pancakes. Be warned, however, that you will have the family queueing up to eat them, so it's just as well to make a double quantity if they are hungry. Scotch pancakes should be served warm, more or less straight from the pan, spread with butter and sprinkled with sugar.

scotch pancakes
with butter and caster sugar

100 g self-raising flour

a pinch of salt

1 egg

25 g caster sugar, plus extra to serve

125 ml milk

40 g butter, plus extra to serve

makes 12–15

Put the flour and salt in a large mixing bowl, make a dip in the centre and add the egg, sugar and milk. Melt 25 g of the butter in a small saucepan, then add to the mixing bowl. Work the mixture together with a wire whisk or wooden spoon to make a smooth batter. Beat for 1 minute, then set aside for 10 minutes.

Set a heavy-based frying pan or griddle over medium heat, add the remaining butter and when it melts, swish it around the pan, then pour off the excess into a small heatproof bowl. Put the pan back on the heat and spoon 1 tablespoon of the batter into the pan – this will naturally form a small, circular pancake. Cook until the pancake browns and bubbles appear on the surface, then turn it over using a palette knife or fish slice. Remove onto a warm tea towel and wrap loosely to keep warm. Cook the remaining pancake mixture in batches, returning a little of the melted butter back to the pan as necessary.

Serve immediately, spread with butter and sprinkled with caster sugar.

Variation For small children, make Mickey or Minnie Mouse pancakes. Spoon 1 tablespoon of the pancake mixture into the centre of a heavy-based hot frying pan, then dot 2 teaspoons of pancake mixture close to the edge of the circle to form ear shapes.

Pain au chocolat has really taken off outside France over the last 20 years, but less well known are Italian savoury *cornetti* (croissants), stuffed with mozzarella and prosciutto or cooked ham. I used to eat them for breakfast in a Roman bar close to the Pantheon on my way to work every morning. Now, back in the UK, I am forced to make my own with a pack of instant croissant dough.

instant savoury croissants

1 pack of ready-to-bake croissant dough
4 paper-thin slices of cooked or Parma ham, about 400 g
1 teaspoon dried oregano
1 teaspoon sun-dried tomato paste
150 g mozzarella or Emmenthal cheese
freshly ground black pepper

makes 8

Open the croissant dough following the instructions on the packet. Lay the sheets of dough on a work surface.

Cut each slice of ham into 2 triangles. Put a triangle of ham on each triangle of dough, sprinkle with a little oregano and black pepper and add a tiny blob of sun-dried tomato paste. Put a strip of mozzarella on the long edge of the triangle and roll the dough around the cheese, bending the roll to form a crescent shape. Transfer to a baking sheet and cook in a preheated oven at 180ºC (350ºF) Gas 4 for 10 minutes or until golden. Serve warm.

Variation Try anchovy fillets instead of ham or, for a vegetarian version, replace the ham with chopped tomato.

grannie's scones

with whipped cream and strawberries

My mother's scones were the best. I'm not even sure they should be called scones, as they are different from everybody else's – they are more cake than bread, with a crumbly texture and a golden colour. She used to make them just before we got home from school and they would be cooling on a wire rack, ready to split open and fill with butter and jam and take outside into the garden.

200 g self-raising flour
1 teaspoon bicarbonate of soda
1 teaspoon cream of tartar
a pinch of salt
25 g chilled butter, diced
25 g caster sugar
2 eggs
80–100 ml sour milk

to serve
strawberry jam
125 ml whipped cream
small strawberries
icing sugar

straight-sided scone cutter, 6 cm diameter

makes 8

Sieve the flour, bicarbonate of soda, cream of tartar and salt into a mixing bowl. Add the butter and rub it into the flour evenly with your fingertips, then mix in the sugar. Add 1 of the eggs and the milk and, using a knife, work the dough into a ball quickly and lightly. The dough should be soft, moist and malleable.

Transfer the dough to a floured work surface, then flatten it with your hands and shape into a circle, about 2–3 cm thick. If the dough is too moist, add a little extra flour. Cut out as many scones as the dough allows. Roll the trimmings into a ball, flatten it and cut out a couple more scones. Shape the remaining trimmings into 1 single scone. Transfer the scones to a baking sheet. Beat the remaining egg in a small bowl, then brush the scones with it. Bake in a preheated oven at 200ºC (400ºF) Gas 6 for 10–15 minutes until well risen and golden.

While still warm, split the scones open, spread with jam, add a spoon of whipped cream and top with a strawberry. Sprinkle with sifted icing sugar.

picnics

A day in the open air is an exhilarating way to unwind. Pack up everything you need and escape to your favourite place and do nothing but luxuriate in the great outdoors all day. Take plenty to eat – dips, vegetables sticks and filled loaves are easy and filling options and seasonal fare, like cherries, are perfect to nibble on. For a memorable feast, take a tart or pie straight from the oven and bake a cake or muffins to have with a flask of tea in the afternoon.

primavera tart

Primavera is Italian for spring and is often used to describe risottos and pasta sauces made with a selection of early summer vegetables. I have used courgette, tomato and asparagus enhanced with fresh basil, but chopped baby carrots, peas, broad beans and green beans would work well. Because asparagus is delicate and looks good, I have cooked it separately and put it on top of the filling, but you could use paper-thin strips of pancetta instead.

To make the pastry, put the flours, sifted icing sugar and salt in a bowl, then add the butter, egg yolks and wine. Quickly and lightly knead the ingredients together into a smooth ball. Wrap in clingfilm and chill in the refrigerator for 1 hour.

Meanwhile, to make the filling, melt the butter in a heavy-based frying pan, then add the onion and parsley and cook until the onion is soft, without allowing it to colour. Add the tomatoes and cook for 10 minutes, then add the courgettes, basil, salt and pepper and stir-fry for 3 minutes or until the courgettes are tender but still firm. Leave to cool.

Sprinkle a clean work surface and rolling pin with plenty of flour. Set the pastry in the centre of the flour, then flatten it with the palm of your hand and shape it into a neat circle. Take the rolling pin and roll the pastry one way, then give it a quarter turn and roll it the other way, shaping the dough back into a circle with your hands from time to time. Continue until the pastry is about 4 cm larger than the tart tin.

Roll the pastry loosely around the rolling pin and transfer it carefully to the greased tin. Open it out and smooth it to line the tin, pressing it into the corners. Put the baking parchment on top and fill with the baking beans. Bake in a preheated oven at 220°F (425°C) Gas 7 for 10 minutes. Remove the baking beans and the parchment, then reduce the oven temperature to 180°C (350°C) Gas 4.

Meanwhile, cook the asparagus in salted boiling water for about 10 minutes until tender. The cooking time will depend on the quality of the asparagus, so taste before draining.

Pour the courgette mixture into the pastry case and spread evenly. Arrange the asparagus tips on top, like spokes on a wheel, with the tips pointing outwards. Put the eggs, cream, Parmesan and plenty of salt and pepper in a small bowl and whisk well. Pour over the courgette mixture and return to the oven for 20 minutes.

If you are going on a picnic immediately, leave to cool slightly in the tin, wrap in aluminium foil and transfer to a picnic box. Otherwise, leave to cool competely, wrap in foil and refrigerate until required. Don't forget to take a pastry slice and plate.

50 g butter

2 onions, finely chopped

a handful of fresh parsley, finely chopped

800 g canned tomatoes, drained, deseeded and chopped

500 g small courgettes, sliced

a handful of fresh basil leaves, chopped

10 asparagus spears, trimmed

3 eggs

5 tablespoons double cream

40 g Parmesan cheese, grated

sea salt and freshly ground black pepper

pastry

150 g plain flour

15 g cornflour

10 g icing sugar

a pinch of salt

90 g butter, softened

2 small egg yolks

1 tablespoon dry white wine or iced water

a loose-based tart tin, 26 cm diameter, greased

a circle of baking parchment, 34 cm diameter

serves 6–8

Of all the pies in this section, this is the simplest and quickest to make, and probably looks and tastes the most exotic. I used a jar of ready-made pesto, but if you make your own pesto it will be even more delicious. I first made it as an Easter treat and it went down so well that it has since become a firm favourite for festive occasions and picnics. It also works well with white fish instead of salmon.

layered salmon, prawn and potato filo pie

500 g new potatoes

800 g canned tomatoes, drained, deseeded
  and chopped

2 garlic cloves, crushed

1 small piece of dried chilli, to taste

500 g salmon fillet, skin removed, cut lengthways
  into medium-sized chunks

100–150 g ready-made basil pesto

100 g butter, melted

6 large sheets of filo pastry

200 g cooked peeled prawns

sea salt and freshly ground black pepper

olive oil, for frying

green salad, to serve

a springform cake tin, 22 cm diameter

serves 6–8

Cook the potatoes in salted boiling water for 20–30 minutes or until tender, drain and leave to cool.

Heat enough olive oil to cover the base of a large saucepan over medium heat. Add the tomatoes, garlic and chilli, reduce the heat to low, then cover and simmer for 30 minutes, stirring from time to time to ensure the sauce does not stick. Mash the tomatoes to a pulp using a potato masher. Season the salmon with salt and pepper, then add to the saucepan for 1–2 minutes to lightly cook. Transfer the sauce to a bowl and leave to cool. Slice the potatoes lengthways, then put in a bowl with the pesto and toss to coat evenly.

Brush the base and sides of the cake tin with a little of the melted butter. Brush a sheet of filo pastry with melted butter and lay it across the cake tin to line the base and sides of the tin, leaving any excess hanging over the sides. Brush another sheet of filo pastry with butter and lay it at right angles to the first sheet, smoothing it down to line the base and sides of the tin. There should now be an equal overhang of filo all the way round the tin. Repeat with the remaining sheets of pastry, reserving a little of the butter.

Cover the base of the pie with half the potato mixture, followed by half the sauce and half the prawns. Make a second layer of each and then carefully fold the overhang of pastry over the filling. Brush the top of the pie with the remaining melted butter.

Set the tin on a baking sheet and cook in a preheated oven at 200ºC (400ºF) Gas 6 for 25 minutes until golden brown.

If you are going on a picnic immediately, leave to cool slightly in the tin, then wrap in a clean tea towel. Otherwise, leave to cool completely, wrap in aluminium foil and refrigerate until required. Don't forget to take a sharp knife and platter for serving. Serve with a green salad.

In Sicily, this is known as *Cabbucio*, meaning hood or cowl, and refers to a kind of bruschetta with a lid. Authentic Italian bread is still additive-free, which means it goes stale quickly, but put yesterday's uncut loaf in a hot oven for a few minutes and it will come out like new. Cut it open while hot and anoint it with extra virgin oil and your chosen filling and you have a delicious snack. Alternatively, you can use fresh bread.

hot crusty loaf
filled with mozzarella, salami and tomato

500 g bloomer or other fresh 'flat'
    crusty Italian loaf

5 large tomatoes, thinly sliced

200 g mozzarella or primo sole cheese,
    thinly sliced

100 g sliced salami or Parma ham, or
    whole anchovy fillets

a small bunch of oregano or basil

sea salt and freshly ground black pepper

extra virgin olive oil, for drizzling

serves 4

Heat the bread in a preheated oven at 220ºC (425ºF) Gas 7 for 5 minutes. While the bread is still hot, cut it in half lengthways and make small incisions all over the cut surfaces of both halves of the bread. Drizzle with olive oil and sprinkle with salt, pepper and half the oregano leaves. On the bottom half of the loaf, put a layer of tomato, followed by a layer of cheese. Top with the salami and the remaining oregano leaves. Sandwich the 2 halves together, then wrap in aluminium foil and a clean tea towel, and transfer it to a picnic basket. Don't forget to take a bread knife and chopping board.

Focaccia is the flat, soft springy olive oil bread from Liguria, classically topped with rosemary, olive oil and coarse salt. In this recipe, it is rolled thinly to make it crusty. As with all bread recipes, it takes time to make and prove, so this is not a dish to make in a hurry but, if you can spare the time, it is well worth the effort. This delicious pie can be adapted for vegetarians, by omitting the cured meats and adding some other tangy ingredients such as olives, capers or anchovies.

roast pepper, mozzarella and Italian cured meat focaccia pie

3 peppers, preferably 1 red, 1 orange and 1 yellow, halved, deseeded and cut into 8 strips

2 garlic cloves, finely chopped

a handful of fresh parsley, finely chopped

400 g canned whole plum tomatoes, drained, deseeded and chopped

125 g mozzarella cheese, thinly sliced

120 g dry cured meats, such as bresaola or prosciutto

1–2 teaspoons dried oregano

sea salt and freshly ground black pepper

olive oil, for frying

focaccia dough

300 g 00 Italian flour

300 g semolina

10 g dried yeast

10 g sea salt

5 tablespoons extra virgin olive oil, plus extra for oiling, brushing and drizzling

300 ml warm water

coarse sea salt, for sprinkling

a circular baking sheet, 30 cm diameter, oiled

a small blanket or a sheet of bubble wrap

serves 8–12

Heat plenty of olive oil to cover the base of a large pan, add the peppers, garlic, parsley, salt and pepper and stir well until it starts to bubble, then reduce the heat, cover and simmer for 25 minutes or until tender. Leave to cool.

To make the dough, put the flours, yeast, salt, olive oil and warm water in a large mixing bowl. Work the ingredients together into a ball with your hands and then transfer to a clean floured work surface. To knead the dough, pull it into an oval shape, anchor the end nearest to you with your left fist and push the dough away from you with the base of your right fist, putting the full weight of your body behind your hand. When the dough is fully extended, roll it back up on itself and towards you with your fingers. Give the dough roll a quarter turn and repeat. Go on repeating this until the dough is smooth, soft and springy. This will take about 30 minutes. Alternatively, put the ingredients in a food processor and process for 5–10 minutes until smooth, soft and springy.

Transfer the dough to a large oiled mixing bowl, cover with clingfilm and wrap in a blanket or in bubble wrap, then set in a warm, draught-free spot for 20 minutes, during which time the dough should double in size.

Knock back (punch) the dough for a couple of minutes to remove the air and then divide into 3 pieces. Knead the 3 pieces of dough into smooth balls. Sprinkle a clean work surface and rolling pin with plenty of flour. Set one of the dough balls in the centre of the flour, then flatten it with the palm of your hand and shape it into a neat circle. Take the rolling pin and roll the pastry one way, then give it a quarter turn and roll it the other way, shaping the dough with your hands from time to time. Continue until the pastry is the same size as the baking sheet. Transfer the dough to the baking sheet and cover with the tomatoes, mozzarella and cured meats, leaving a border of 1–2 cm around the edge. Sprinkle with the oregano and drizzle with olive oil.

Roll out a second circle of dough and put this on top of the cured meats. Cover this with the peppers. Roll a third circle of dough and put this on top.

Carefully press down the edges of the pie to seal them together and prick them with a fork all the way around. Then prick the pie all over right through to the tin base. Brush the top with olive oil, sprinkle with coarse salt and cook in a preheated oven at 180ºC (350ºF) Gas 4 for 45 minutes.

If you are going on a picnic immediately, wrap the focaccia and the baking sheet in a large tea towel and a small blanket. Otherwise, leave to cool, wrap in aluminium foil and refrigerate until required. Don't forget to take a bread knife and chopping board.

Two more ideas on a theme. The Rustic Loaf Filled with Ham and Apple Chutney is quintessentially British, conjuring up the memories of harvest-time picnics in the hay fields in days gone by, while the Ciabatta Bread Filled with Roasted Peppers, Jerusalem Hoummus and Rocket steps straight into the 21st century, summoning up the city sandwich bar. The former can be made with hot, home-cooked ham and fresh bread, or straight from the supermarket with cold sliced ham and hot bread. The latter is a vegetarian treat that everyone will want to eat and, if you can bear it, it is well worth peeling the peppers, as it gives them a rich, fleshy texture.

rustic loaf
filled with ham and apple chutney

1 kg gammon joint
1 bay leaf
2 x 250 g rustic loaves
2–3 tablespoons mayonnaise
100 g shredded iceberg lettuce
2 tablespoons apple chutney

serves 4

Soak the gammon joint in cold water for several hours. Discard the soaking water and transfer the gammon to a large pan. Fill with fresh cold water, add the bay leaf and slowly bring to the boil . Reduce the heat and simmer for 40 minutes, turning once. Leave to stand in the water for 20 minutes. Transfer the gammon to a carving tray and thinly slice 400 g of the ham.

Cut one of the loaves in half lengthways and spread the halves with mayonnaise. Cover the bottom half with lettuce and half the sliced ham, then spread evenly with chutney. Sandwich the 2 halves together, then repeat with the remaining ingredients. Wrap in aluminium foil and a clean tea towel, then transfer to a picnic basket. Don't forget to take a bread knife and chopping board.

ciabatta bread
filled with roasted peppers, jerusalem hoummus and rocket

2 red peppers, halved and deseeded
2 yellow peppers, halved and deseeded
8 sprigs of rosemary
2 x 250 g ciabatta loaves
150–175 g Jerusalem Hoummus (page 85) or
　　ready-made hoummus
2 large handfuls of rocket
extra virgin olive oil, for drizzling

serves 4

Put the pepper halves in a roasting tin and put a sprig of rosemary and a little olive oil inside each one. Cook in a preheated oven at 220ºC (425ºF) Gas 7 for 25 minutes or until tender. Leave until cool enough to handle, then discard the rosemary and peel the pepper halves.

Put the loaves in the oven for 5 minutes to heat though. Cut in half lengthways and spread the halves with the hoummus. Cover the bottom halves with rocket and the peppers, then sandwich the bread together. Wrap in aluminium foil and a clean tea towel, then transfer to a picnic basket. Don't forget to take a bread knife and a chopping board.

avocado, olive and anchovy dip

Like most recipes made with avocado, the pale creamy green colour of this tangy Spanish dip darkens to khaki quite quickly, so it is best made shortly before you eat it. Try burying the avocado stone in the dip, as this is supposed to prevent discolouration.

1 large avocado, peeled, stoned and cut into chunks
4 anchovy fillets, halved
1 garlic clove, crushed
1 tablespoon ready-made olive pesto
1 tablespoon extra virgin olive oil
2 tablespoons freshly squeezed lemon juice
1 tablespoon chopped fresh parsley, plus extra to serve
a large pinch of sugar
freshly ground black pepper

serves 2–4

Put the ingredients in a food processor and reduce to a smooth dipping consistency. Transfer to a serving bowl, cover and refrigerate until required.

When ready to serve, sprinkle with parsley.

aubergine and tahini dip

This Middle Eastern meze is cool, mild and refreshing. Baked whole in a microwave or oven, the flesh of the aubergine becomes silky smooth. As well as being mixed into a dip, baked aubergine is also delicious chopped and dressed with extra virgin olive oil, seasoning and fresh herbs for a delicate starter or salad.

1 medium-sized aubergine, about 150 g
1 garlic clove, crushed
1 tablespoon freshly squeezed lemon juice
3 tablespoons extra virgin olive oil, plus extra to serve
1 tablespoon dark tahini paste
sea salt

to serve

a handful of fresh parsley, finely chopped
1 tablespoon black olives

serves 2–4

Prick the aubergine a few times with a fork and set on a piece of kitchen paper in a microwave oven. Cook on HIGH for 3 minutes, then turn and cook for 3 minutes more. Alternatively, bake in a preheated oven at 180ºC (350ºF) Gas 4 for 20–30 minutes until soft.

Leave until cool enough to handle, then peel. Cut into 3 or 4 slices and leave to drain between 2 sheets of kitchen paper.

Transfer to a food processor with the garlic, lemon juice, olive oil and tahini paste. Add salt to taste, then spoon into a serving dish, cover and refrigerate until required.

When ready to serve, sprinkle with parsley and olives and drizzle with olive oil.

cream cheese, walnut and celery dip

This tasty combination is a Western classic. Try hazelnuts or blue cheese for a change.

200 g cream cheese
100 g walnut pieces
2 tablespoons boiling water
1 tablespoon olive oil
2 tender celery sticks, finely chopped
sea salt and freshly ground black pepper

serves 2–4

Put the cheese, walnuts, water, olive oil, salt and pepper in a food processor and reduce to a dipping consistency. Transfer to a bowl and stir in the celery. Cover and chill until required.

jerusalem hoummus
with toasted pine nuts

The addition of coriander and pine nuts gives aroma and texture to hoummus.

420 g canned chickpeas, drained, rinsed and dried
1 garlic clove, crushed
freshly squeezed juice of 1 lemon
2 tablespoons extra virgin olive oil
2 tablespoons dark tahini paste
½ teaspoon sea salt
3 tablespoons chopped fresh coriander
3 tablespoons pine nuts, toasted in a dry frying pan

serves 2–4

Put the chickpeas, garlic, lemon juice, olive oil, tahini paste, salt and 4 tablespoons of water in a food processor and reduce to a dipping consistency. Transfer to a bowl. Stir in most of the coriander and pine nuts. Sprinkle with the remaining coriander and pine nuts, then serve.

This is an eye-catching Catalan salad that I discovered in Barcelona. The hard-boiled eggs looked stunning placed in neat lines on top of the lentils. Each one was artfully dressed with a swirl of anchovy, short chive plumes and small mint leaves, giving them the appearance of tiny wedding hats. As this would be difficult to transport on a picnic, you may prefer to simply stir the herbs into the lentils and scatter the eggs and anchovies on top. Meat eaters may like to boil the lentils in water previously used for cooking ham, as it gives them extra depth of flavour.

400 g dried Puy lentils

1 garlic clove, very thinly sliced

a handful of fresh mint, plus extra to serve

a handful of fresh coriander or parsley, plus extra to serve

a handful of fresh chives, finely snipped

4 hard-boiled eggs, chopped

8 anchovy fillets

olive oil, for frying

dressing

1 tablespoon red wine vinegar

3 tablespoons extra virgin olive oil

1 teaspoon mustard powder

1 teaspoon sugar

sea salt and freshly ground black pepper

serves 4

herbed lentil salad

with hard-boiled eggs and anchovies

Cook the lentils in boiling water for 25 minutes, then drain. Cover the base of a large saucepan with olive oil, add the garlic and heat gently. When the garlic starts to colour, discard it. Add the lentils and toss until well coated, then leave to cool a little.

To make the dressing, put the vinegar, olive oil, mustard powder, sugar, salt and pepper in a screw-top jar. Seal and shake well.

Chop the mint and coriander together finely, then add to the lentils with the chives and dressing and mix well. Transfer to a plastic container with a lid, then crumble the egg on top and scatter over the anchovies. Sprinkle with mint and coriander before serving.

Variation Use boiled rice or couscous rather than lentils.

500 g freshly cooked chicken meat, cut into strips

1 small ripe mango, peeled, stoned and cut into
     1–2 cm cubes

1 large slice of ripe melon, peeled, deseeded and cut
     into 1–2 cm cubes

100 g seedless grapes, halved

2 tablespoons finely chopped celery

200 ml mayonnaise

freshly squeezed juice of ½ lemon, plus 1 tablespoon
     to serve

½ teaspoon mixed mustard seeds

½ teaspoon cumin seeds

½ teaspoon coriander seeds

2 teaspoons ground turmeric

¼ teaspoon chilli powder

1 teaspoon ground ginger

2 tablespoons nibbed pistachio nuts

sea salt and freshly ground black pepper, plus
     1 tablespoon to serve

to serve

100 g mixed salad leaves, such as lambs' lettuce,
     baby spinach or radicchio

1 lemon, thinly sliced (optional)

1 tablespoon chopped fresh coriander

serves 4–6

This pretty chicken dish (my take on Coronation Chicken) makes a delicious centrepiece for a special picnic, summer buffet or family meal. The cool fruit contrasts with the creamy texture of the chicken and the spice cuts the rich mayonnaise, making a refreshing dish that can be dressed up or down according to the occasion. Your own freshly roasted or poached chicken will absorb the flavours better than one that has been left to go completely cold. However, you can make a swift version using a ready-cooked chicken and curry powder.

spiced chicken and mango mayonnaise
with pistachio nuts

Put the strips of chicken in a large bowl with the mango, melon, grapes and celery. Add the mayonnaise and lemon juice and mix well. Put the mustard seeds, cumin seeds and coriander seeds in a mortar and grind finely with a pestle. Add to the chicken with the turmeric, chilli powder, ginger, 1 tablespoon of the pistachio nuts, ½ teaspoon salt and some black pepper. Mix well, cover and chill until required.

When ready to serve, arrange the salad leaves around the edge of a serving dish, drizzle with the lemon juice, add salt and pepper and top with lemon slices, if using. Spoon the chicken salad into the middle of the dish and sprinkle with the coriander and the remaining pistachio nuts. Cover closely with clingfilm until ready to serve.

A fresh-tasting tabbouleh salad is a welcome dish on any summer table. In the Lebanon, where it originated, it is served as a starter with hoummus and other meze, and it is also popular for Sunday picnics. This recipe is based on an authentic tabbouleh recipe, but I have added gherkins and horseradish sauce to complement the pastrami. I have also added cherry tomatoes instead of the chopped whole ones traditionally used.

cherry tomato tabbouleh salad
with pastrami

150 g bulghur wheat

2 handfuls of fresh parsley

a handful of fresh mint

a handful of fresh basil

a small bunch of spring onions, finely chopped

1 garlic clove, finely chopped

1 tablespoon cocktail gherkins

250 g firm cherry tomatoes, halved

100 ml olive oil

2 tablespoons freshly squeezed lemon juice

1 tablespoon horseradish (optional)

12 slices of pastrami, about 200 g, to serve

sea salt and freshly ground black pepper

serves 4–6

Put the bulghur wheat in a large bowl, add enough cold water to cover and leave to stand for 30 minutes. Drain if necessary, pat dry on a clean tea towel and transfer to a large bowl. Chop the parsley, mint and basil together and add to the bulghur wheat. Add the spring onions, garlic, gherkins, tomatoes, olive oil, lemon juice, horseradish, if using, and salt and pepper to taste. Cover and leave to stand for a couple of hours to allow the flavours to develop.

When ready to serve, arrange the pastrami around the edge of a serving dish and pile the tabbouleh in the middle. Cover closely with clingfilm until ready to serve.

Variation Serve with smoked fish, broken into pieces or cubed feta or tofu instead of pastrami, if you prefer.

I love homemade cake and the plainer, the better. I have never seen the need for sickly fillings and toppings that mask the flavour. At most, all a good cake needs is a simple frosting, melted chocolate topping or jam in the middle. This freshly baked, moist yet crumbly aromatic pineapple loaf needs no more than a dusting of icing sugar on top. When taking a cake on a picnic, don't forget to put a knife in the tin.

pineapple and thyme loaf cake

150 g unsalted butter or margarine

150 g caster sugar

3 eggs, beaten

75 g self-raising flour

75 g semolina

2 teaspoons baking powder

250 g canned pineapple chunks, chopped in a
    food processor

1 tablespoon finely chopped fresh thyme

15 g vanilla sugar or 1 teaspoon vanilla essence

icing sugar, to dust (optional)

1 kg loaf tin, lined with greaseproof paper

serves 8

Put the butter and sugar in a large mixing bowl and beat until light and fluffy. Add the eggs a little at a time, beating well after each addition; it may be necessary to add a little of the flour to prevent the mixture curdling. Fold in the remaining flour, semolina, baking powder, pineapple, thyme and vanilla sugar.

Bake in a preheated oven at 190°C (375°F) Gas 5 for 30 minutes or until well risen and golden. When the cake is cool enough to handle, turn out onto a cooling rack and leave to cool. Dust with icing sugar, then wrap in aluminium foil and transfer to a tin.

Children of all ages love chocolate muffins and the more chocolatey, the better, so I have added chocolate spread to this recipe to give them extra kid appeal. What better way of getting them to cook than asking them to help you make their favourite treat? Not that it is ever a problem when cake is on the menu – it's keeping their fingers out of the mixing bowl and the mixture off their faces that is the problem. This recipe is so simple to make that older children can make them by themselves.

triple chocolate chip muffins

225 g self-raising flour

2 teaspoons baking powder

25 g cocoa powder

100 g caster sugar

100 g good-quality plain chocolate, chopped

1 egg, beaten

4 tablespoons chocolate and hazelnut spread

6 tablespoons vegetable oil

160 ml milk

12 paper muffin cases

a 12-hole muffin tray

makes 12

Set the paper muffin cases in the tray. Sift the flour, baking powder and cocoa powder into a mixing bowl, then add the sugar, chocolate, egg, chocolate and hazelnut spread, and vegetable oil and mix well with a wooden spoon. Add the milk a little at a time, stirring well between each addition, until the mixture has a good pouring consistency.

Ladle the mixture into the cases and bake in a preheated oven at 200°C (400°F) Gas 6 for 20–25 minutes or until the muffins are well risen and firm to the touch. Transfer to a cooling rack, leave to cool and transfer to a tin until required.

Variation Substitute the chocolate and hazelnut spread with 4 tablespoons of freshly made espresso coffee and the chocolate with 100 g chopped walnuts. Add an extra 50 g of caster sugar and an extra egg to the mixture.

traditional english apple tart

Of all the fancy puddings there are, there is nothing to beat a simple baked apple tart. It's quick and simple to make, delicious and it lends itself perfectly to the picnic basket, hot or cold. Slivers of cheddar cheese go well with it too. Interestingly, it was one of the few English things that I was asked to make when I lived in Italy. Children love small apple pies, which can be made in jam tart tins, but you need to stew the apple to a mush and let it cool before using.

300 g plain flour
a pinch of sea salt
150 g chilled butter, diced
5 tablespoons chilled water
1 kg cooking apples, peeled, cored and thinly sliced
100 g caster sugar, plus extra to decorate and to serve
cream or set yoghurt, to serve

a shallow pie dish, about 26 cm diameter, greased

serves 6

Put the flour, salt and butter in a large mixing bowl and rub in the butter with your fingertips until the mixture resembles fine breadcrumbs. Add the water and work the mixture together to form a dough. This should be done quickly and lightly with your fingertips or the blade of a round-bladed knife. Alternatively, put the ingredients in a food processor and process until the ingredients are reduced to a dough.

Divide the dough in half and work each half into a neat ball. Sprinkle a clean work surface and a rolling pin with plenty of flour. Set 1 of the pastry balls in the centre of the flour, flatten it with the palm of your hand and shape into a neat circle. Roll the pastry one way, then give it a quarter turn and roll it the other way, shaping the dough back into a circle from time to time. Continue until the pastry is slightly larger than the pie dish.

Roll the pastry around the rolling pin and transfer it carefully to the pie dish, open it out and smooth it to line the dish and the border. Fill with the apple slices, then brush the border with water. Roll out the second ball of dough as before and put this on top of the apples. Trim off the excess pastry with a sharp knife. Press down the border with your thumb to seal it, creating a regular pattern around the edge as you do so. Brush the top of the pie with water and sprinkle with caster sugar.

Set the pie on a baking sheet in the centre of the preheated oven and bake at 220°C (425°F) Gas 7 for 20 minutes, then reduce the heat to 150°C (300°F) Gas 2, and bake for 20 minutes more. Check to see if the fruit is cooked by gently pushing a skewer into it. If it offers resistance, it is not cooked, so cook for a further 10 minutes. If you are going on a picnic immediately, allow to cool a little, wrap in a clean tea towel and a small blanket and don't forget a pastry slice. Serve warm or cold with sugar and cream.

elegant al fresco

Whether it is a long leisurely lunch in the shade, a romantic dinner for two or a supper party with friends under the stars, dining outdoors should be every bit as luxurious as a dinner party indoors and will prove more memorable. There is an abundance of fresh produce available in the summer to inspire colourful starters and side dishes, simple meat, fish, pasta and rice dishes, and last but not least luscious, indulgent fruity puddings.

99

This three-in-one starter is substantial enough to serve as a light lunch. It consists of peppers stuffed with mozzarella and anchovy or Parma ham, and mushrooms stuffed with crabmeat, both topped with herbed breadcrumbs and tomatoes with herbed breadcrumbs. The inspiration came from a simple herbed tomato recipe, *pomodori raganati*, that I picked up in Liguria, which goes well on its own or with meat and fish dishes.

trio of stuffed vegetables

2 large tomatoes, halved and deseeded

a handful of fresh parsley

a handful of fresh mint

a handful of fresh basil

75 g soft white breadcrumbs (page 54)

4 garlic cloves, crushed

2 yellow peppers, halved and deseeded, stalks retained

2 medium or large flat mushrooms, stalks discarded

8 anchovy fillets, chopped, or 1 slice of Parma ham, cut into quarters

60 g mozzarella cheese, cut into 4 slices

100 g crabmeat

1 tablespoon mayonnaise

a pinch of chilli powder

2 teaspoons freshly squeezed lemon juice

sea salt and freshly ground black pepper

extra virgin olive oil, for oiling and drizzling

wild rocket, to serve

serves 4

Invert the tomato halves onto a piece of kitchen paper and leave to drain.

Put the herbs, breadcrumbs and garlic in a food processor and finely chop, then add plenty of salt and pepper.

Arrange the cut pepper halves and mushrooms in an oiled roasting tin, cut side up, and season with salt and pepper and a few drops of olive oil.

Divide the anchovies between the pepper halves, put a slice of mozzarella on top and cover with about 25 g of the breadcrumbs.

Put the crabmeat, mayonnaise, chilli powder and lemon juice in a bowl, mix well, then spoon on top of the mushrooms and cover with about 25 g of the breadcrumbs.

Dry the tomato halves carefully with kitchen paper, then add to the roasting tin. Season with salt and pepper, drizzle with a little olive oil, then cover with 25 g of the breadcrumbs. Scatter any remaining breadcrumbs around the vegetables.

Drizzle olive oil over all the vegetables and bake in a preheated oven at 220°C (425 °F) Gas 7 for 20 minutes or until the vegetables are tender and the breadcrumbs crisp on top. Serve with rocket.

Chilled soups are a summer delight that had to be included here. I hovered between two of my favourites, watercress and asparagus, both refreshing in taste and intense in colour, until I saw this combination of flavoursome salad leaves. I was sure they would make a cracking summer soup and they do! Plunging lightly cooked leaves and vegetables into iced water helps preserve their natural fresh green pigment.

chilled spinach, rocket and watercress soup

4 shallots, chopped

2 garlic cloves, chopped

½ nutmeg, grated, plus extra to serve

100 ml white wine

400 ml vegetable stock

250 g mixed spinach, rocket and watercress leaves

200 ml single cream or yoghurt

sea salt and freshly ground black pepper

olive oil, for frying

to serve

4 teaspoons single cream

4 large leaves of wild rocket

serves 4

Heat enough olive oil to cover the base of a frying pan, add the shallots, garlic and nutmeg and fry over low heat until the onions are soft. Add the wine and stock and bring to the boil, then simmer for 10 minutes. Remove from the heat and leave to cool.

Put the spinach, rocket and watercress in a large pan containing 1 litre of lightly salted boiling water, gently submerse the leaves with a spoon and blanch for 60 seconds. Drain and plunge the leaves into a bowl of cold water and ice to chill quickly. Drain and squeeze out the excess water with your hands.

Put the leaves and the soup in a food processor and blend to a smooth consistency. Add the cream and season with salt and pepper to taste. Cover and chill for at least 2 hours or overnight.

Ladle the soup into bowls, feather with cream and serve with rocket leaves and grated nutmeg.

Cichetti are the Venetian answer to tapas. They are served as snacks in all the bars around Venice and go down well at lunchtime with a glass of Prosecco, the local sparkling wine, as you watch the world flood by. Speck is a cured ham, similar to Parma ham, made in the Alto Adige region to the north of the Veneto.

speck and crayfish cichetti
laced with chilli

4 tablespoons mayonnaise

2 teaspoons sun-dried tomato paste

a pinch chilli of powder, plus extra to serve

1 teaspoon freshly squeezed lime juice

finely pared zest of 1 unwaxed lime

1 celery stick, finely chopped

125 g cooked crayfish tails or prawns, shelled

3 thin slices of wholemeal bread

80 g thinly sliced speck or Parma ham

4 small tender lettuce leaves, to serve

butter, for spreading

serves 4

Put the mayonnaise, sun-dried tomato paste, chilli powder and lime juice in a bowl with 1 teaspoon of the lime zest, then stir. Add the celery and crayfish tails and mix well, then cover and leave until required.

When ready to serve, butter the bread slices, trim the crusts and cut each slice into 4 squares.

Using scissors, cut the speck into 12 pieces. Put them on the bread, then spoon the crayfish mixture on top. Scatter over a couple of strands of lime zest and sprinkle with chilli powder. Serve with lettuce leaves.

The combination of monkfish and scallops on a kebab is delicious. They both have solid textures and distinctive flavours. The addition of thinly sliced salami or pancetta adds a crisp saltiness. By cooking kebabs on a baking sheet in the oven rather than under a grill, they do not dry out and the breadcrumbs soak up the juices that would otherwise be lost. Prepare the skewers in advance and cook them at the last minute.

spiked monkfish, scallops and cherry tomatoes in crispy breadcrumbs

2 tablespoons plain flour

400–500 g monkfish or other thick white fish, cut into 12 square chunks

8 small or 4 large raw, shelled scallops, 150–200 g, halved

80 g thinly sliced Milano salami or pancetta, cut into strips

12 cherry tomatoes

2 tablespoons extra virgin olive oil, plus extra for drizzling

4 tablespoons soft white breadcrumbs (page 54)

sea salt and freshly ground black pepper

to serve

balsamic vinegar

Lemon Roast Potato Wedges (page 121; optional)

rocket and cos lettuce salad

4 metal skewers

serves 4

Put the flour in a large bowl and season with salt and pepper. Add the fish chunks and scallops and shake the bowl until they are well coated with flour.

Wrap the monkfish in the salami strips. Thread the monkfish pieces, scallops and tomatoes onto the skewers, starting and finishing with a tomato.

Oil the base of a rectangular roasting tin with the olive oil. Roll the kebabs in the oil one at a time, then arrange them in the roasting tin. Sprinkle the breadcrumbs on and around the kebabs and then drizzle with more olive oil.

Cook in a preheated oven at 220ºC (425ºF) Gas 7 for 10 minutes or until the fish is set and the breadcrumbs golden. Remove the roasting tin from the oven and drizzle balsamic vinegar over the kebabs. Serve with lemon roast potato wedges, if liked, and a rocket and cos lettuce salad.

Salmon is a great summer standby and not in any way the luxury it once was. A whole cooked salmon makes a magnificent centrepiece for a summer party, but take care not to overcook it. The general rule of cooking fish applies – undercook it and leave it to stand for a few minutes and it will finish cooking in its own heat without drying out. This rich tangy topping can be prepared well in advance and the salmon can be cooked at the last minute. This crumble can also be served cold.

salmon, mascarpone, caper and sun-dried tomato crumble

Put the capers, sun-dried tomatoes and parsley on a chopping board and chop together finely. Put the mascarpone cheese in a bowl and add the chopped caper mixture.

Put the flour and the butter in a bowl and rub in the butter with your fingertips until the mixture resembles fine breadcrumbs. Add salt and pepper and stir in the lemon zest. Cover and refrigerate until required.

Arrange the salmon pieces in an oiled roasting tin, season with salt and pepper and drizzle with the lemon juice. Spread the mascarpone cheese mixture on the top of the salmon and sprinkle with the crumble. Cook in a preheated oven at 220ºC (425ºF) Gas 7 for 10 minutes until the salmon is just set and the crumble is crisp and golden. Transfer to a serving plate and serve with lemon wedges, French beans and new potatoes tossed in olive oil and mint, if liked.

*Note You can use capers in brine rather than salted capers, but you will need to add a pinch of salt to the mascarpone cheese mixture.

Variation To prepare a whole side of salmon, line a long roasting tin with baking parchment, place the salmon on top and proceed as above. Cook for 20–30 minutes until golden on top, then leave to rest for 10 minutes before serving.

2 tablespoons salted capers, rinsed
    and dried*
20 g soft sun-dried tomatoes
a large handful of fresh parsley
175 g mascarpone cheese
40 g plain flour
20 g butter
finely chopped zest and freshly
    squeezed juice of ½ unwaxed lemon
4 salmon fillets, about 500 g
sea salt and freshly ground black pepper
extra virgin olive oil, for oiling

to serve
lemon wedges
French beans
boiled new potatoes tossed in olive oil
    and chopped fresh mint (optional)

serves 4

This quick version of *spaghetti ai frutti di mare* is a great recipe for a summer dinner party. The tomato sauce can be made in advance, the spaghetti cooked at the last minute, the seafood added and then everything put together and served. Make sure you use fine spaghettini rather than the thicker spaghetti, as it cooks more quickly and you'll be surprised at the difference it makes to the lightness of the dish. I always stock up on good dried Italian pasta whenever I see it, which generally means on a visit to an Italian store. The sauce would also work well in a risotto.

instant seafood spaghetti

1 kg canned plum tomatoes, drained and deseeded, juice reserved

5 tablespoons extra virgin olive oil, plus extra to serve

4 garlic cloves, chopped

1 small piece of fresh chilli, to taste

100 g mixed, cooked seafood, such as squid rings, prawns, mussels or clams

2 tablespoons finely chopped fresh flat leaf parsley, plus extra to serve

500 g spaghettini

sea salt and freshly ground black pepper

serves 4

Put the tomatoes, olive oil, garlic and chilli in a heavy-based saucepan, cover and simmer over low heat for 30 minutes or until the tomatoes are reduced to a creamy mass. Stir from time to time to ensure the sauce does not stick to the bottom of the pan. Add a little of the reserved tomato juice to keep the sauce moist, if necessary. Discard the chilli and reduce the sauce to a smooth pulp using a potato masher.

Add the seafood, parsley and plenty of black pepper to the saucepan and simmer very gently. Meanwhile, cook the spaghettini in plenty of salted boiling water, following the instructions on the packet, until al dente. Drain immediately, reserving 2 tablespoons of the cooking water, and return to the cooking pan.

Add the sauce and the reserved cooking water to the pasta pan and mix until the sauce is well distributed. Transfer to a serving dish, sprinkle with parsley and black pepper and drizzle with olive oil. Serve immediately.

Variation Add 2 drained cans of clams or tuna fish to the tomato sauce instead of the mixed seafood.

This delicious combination of chicken and caramelized peaches originated in Iran and the addition of nibbed pistachio nuts fits in with its Middle Eastern origins. Nibbed pistachio nuts are prepared for use in confectionery and are generally sold in Middle Eastern stores. They are fantastic for use in all kinds of dishes because the skin is removed, revealing that distinctive pistachio green. This dish can be prepared in advance and simply reheated when required, adding the extra fruit and nuts just before serving.

spiced chicken
with pistachios and caramelized peaches

8 chicken thighs, skin on

125 ml chicken stock

1 onion, finely chopped

2 tablespoons ground turmeric

2 teaspoons ground cinnamon

2 tablespoons grappa or vodka

3 peaches or kiwi fruit, peeled, stoned and quartered

freshly squeezed juice of 1 lime or lemon

1 tablespoon brown sugar

1 tablespoon chopped or nibbed pistachio nuts,
    plus extra to serve

sea salt and freshly ground black pepper

olive oil, for frying

to serve

1 peach or 2 kiwi fruit, peeled, stoned and
    sliced (optional)

boiled rice

serves 4

Rub the chicken pieces with plenty of salt and pepper. Heat enough oil to cover the base of a large frying pan and fry the chicken pieces over high heat until golden on all sides. Transfer to a plate.

Pour off the excess fat from the frying pan and reserve. Add the stock to the pan and set it over low heat to deglaze, then scrape up the juices and reserve. Return 2 tablespoons of chicken fat to the pan and add the onion, turmeric and cinnamon, mix well and cook over low heat until the onion is soft.

Increase the heat and return the chicken to the pan. Turn once or twice in the onion mixture, add the grappa and continue to cook until it has evaporated. Pour the stock back into the pan, cover and cook for 20 minutes. Turn the chicken and simmer again for 20 minutes.

Heat 1 tablespoon of olive oil over low heat, then add the peaches and cook for 1 minute. Add the lime juice and sugar and simmer for 1 minute. Add the pistachio nuts, stir gently, then cover and cook for 20 minutes.

Transfer to a serving dish and scatter over extra pistachio nuts and peach slices, if using. Serve with boiled rice.

Roast guinea fowl is a treat; half chicken, half game, it is full of flavour. Where we might roast whole birds and quite large pieces, Italians tend to cut poultry and meat into small pieces that roast very quickly and absorb other ingredients more directly, giving great finger-licking potential. This recipe makes for a quick, easy and exotic roast to serve for a special meal. Adding the ready-boiled potatoes and beans to the meat in the cooking pan and mixing them up means that none of the meat juices will be wasted.

italian roast guinea fowl
with new potatoes and green beans

1.5 kg guinea fowl
30 g butter
750 g new potatoes
200 g green beans
100 ml vegetable stock
sea salt
Radicchio Plumes (page 121), to serve

serves 4–6

If using a whole guinea fowl, cut them in half lengthways, then cut each half into 6 evenly sized pieces.

Arrange the guinea fowl in a large roasting tin, dot with butter and sprinkle generously with salt. Cover with aluminium foil and leave to stand at room temperature for 1 hour. Remove the foil, put the pan in the middle of a preheated oven and roast at 200°C (400°F) Gas 6 for 30 minutes or until golden brown and tender, turning at least once.

Meanwhile, put the potatoes in a small saucepan of salted water and boil until tender, then drain. Cook the beans in the same way for about 8 minutes until al dente, then drain.

Add the potatoes and beans to the roasting dish and stir well to coat with the pan juices. Transfer the meat and vegetables to a serving plate.

Deglaze the tin with the stock, boil until reduced by half, then pour over the meat and vegetables. Serve with radicchio plumes.

Variation Free-range chicken or rabbit are also good cooked in this simple, quick and delicious way.

Steak is everybody's favourite, but beware, as it can sometimes be tough. Fillet steak is always reliable, but other steaks, however good in flavour, can vary. I find freezing steak for a few days prior to use helps. The art of cooking a good steak is to have the pan very hot before you put the meat in and to add the oil or butter at the same time as the meat. This way, the minute the meat makes contact with the pan, it will sear the outside, capturing all the juices inside.

fanned steak
with rocket crème fraîche

2 tablespoons olive oil, plus extra to serve
4 fillet steaks, about 600 g, or 4 rump steaks, about 800 g
1 garlic clove, unpeeled and halved
sea salt and freshly ground black pepper

rocket crème fraîche
50 g wild rocket
1 teaspoon mixed mustard seeds, crushed
2 garlic cloves, cut into 3 pieces
150 ml crème fraîche or sour cream
sea salt and freshly ground black pepper

to serve
Lemon Roast Potato Wedges (page 121)
cherry tomatoes
wild rocket leaves

serves 4

To make the rocket crème fraîche, put the rocket, mustard seeds and garlic in a food processor and chop finely. Put the crème fraîche in a mixing bowl and stir in the rocket mixture. Add ½ teaspoon salt and pepper to taste.

Put a large frying pan over medium heat. When the pan is hot, increase the heat and add the olive oil and the steak at the same time. Sear quickly on both sides until dark brown for rare steak. For medium or well-done steak, reduce the heat to medium and cook for a further 2–6 minutes, according to taste.

Transfer the steaks to a chopping board and rub both sides of the meat with the cut garlic and sprinkle with salt. Cut the steak diagonally into 5 or 6 slices.

Arrange a fan of sliced steak on each plate and sprinkle with black pepper and drizzle with olive oil. Serve immediately with the rocket crème fraîche, lemon roast potato wedges, cherry tomatoes and rocket leaves.

Variation Serve the steak on char-grilled ciabatta bread spread with the rocket fraîche, topped with a tomato and some rocket.

Made with almonds, basil and tomato, this pesto recipe comes from Trapane in Sicily, where it is known as *pesto trapanese*. It is traditionally served with a regional pasta called *busiate*, which is similar to *bucatini*. The rich smoky flavour of toasted almonds and the peppery flavour of the basil permeate the risotto rice, making the perfect combination. It is highly recommended for non-vegetarians as well.

risotto with sicilian pesto

2 shallots, finely chopped

500 g risotto rice, preferably vialone nano

60 ml white wine

1 litre hot vegetable stock

extra virgin olive oil, for frying, plus extra to serve

sicilian pesto

75 g toasted sliced almonds

80 g fresh basil leaves

4 garlic cloves, lightly crushed

800 g canned whole plum tomatoes drained, deseeded and chopped

125 ml olive oil

75 g freshly grated pecorino cheese

sea salt and freshly ground black pepper

to serve

toasted sliced almonds

freshly grated pecorino cheese

serves 4

To make the pesto, put the almonds in a food processor with a pinch of salt and grind finely. Transfer to a large bowl.

Put the basil, garlic and tomato in a food processor and reduce to a paste. Add to the ground almonds and stir in the olive oil, pecorino cheese and a good grinding of salt and pepper to taste. Mix well and leave to rest for at least 2 hours.

Cover the base of a large, heavy-based pan with olive oil, heat gently and add the shallots and 2 tablespoons of water. Cook until the shallots are transparent. Add the rice, increase the heat and cook for 2 minutes, stirring continuously. Add the wine and let it evaporate, then reduce the heat.

Level the rice and carefully spoon 10 ladles of freshly boiled stock over the rice, cover with a lid and cook on low heat for 15 minutes. After this time, add the pesto and mix energetically for 1 minute. Turn off the heat, cover and leave to stand for 4–5 minutes.

Transfer the risotto to a serving dish or individual plates, then drizzle with olive oil and sprinkle with almond slices. Serve immediately with pecorino cheese.

Note If ready-toasted sliced almonds are not available, put untoasted sliced almonds on a heavy baking sheet and bake in a preheated oven at 100°C (200°F) Gas Low for 40 minutes or until golden brown. Remove from the sheet and leave to cool before grinding.

I love vegetables of every kind, not least of all because they come and go with the seasons. Summer vegetables, such as new potatoes, young carrots, peas, runner beans and broad beans, need little more than rapid cooking in salted water, with perhaps the addition of a little butter or olive oil, black pepper and a few chopped herbs. However, if you are just going to serve one single vegetable to accompany a meal, here are some simple ways of enhancing them.

french beans
with tomato and garlic

250 g French beans, trimmed
1 tablespoon extra virgin olive oil
1 garlic clove, finely chopped
2 whole canned plum tomatoes, drained, deseeded
    and chopped
sea salt and freshly ground black pepper

serves 4

Boil the beans in a saucepan of lightly salted water until cooked al dente, then drain. Heat the olive oil in a small saucepan over medium heat, add the garlic and tomato and cook until it starts to sizzle. Add the beans, reduce the heat and continue to cook for 5 minutes, stirring from time to time. Add salt and pepper to taste. Serve hot or cold.

Variation Try cooking broccoli, asparagus and broad beans this way.

lemon roast potato
wedges

4 medium potatoes, cut into 8 wedges each
freshly squeezed juice of ½ lemon
1–2 tablespoons extra virgin olive oil
sea salt and freshly ground black pepper

serves 4

Put the potato wedges in a roasting tin, add the lemon juice and season with salt and pepper. Drizzle with the olive oil and stir well. Cook in a preheated oven at 220°C (425°F) Gas 7 for 20–30 minutes until crisp and golden, turning once or twice. Transfer to a serving dish and serve.

Variation When the potatoes are ready, add 250 g cherry tomatoes pricked with the point of a knife, then stir into the potatoes and return to the oven for 5 minutes or until the tomato skins start to split.

radicchio plumes

2 heads of radicchio or chicory, quartered
2 tablespoons extra virgin olive oil, plus extra to serve
sea salt and freshly ground black pepper

a ridged stove-top grill pan

serves 4

Arrange the radicchio quarters, cut side up, on a plate. Dress with the olive oil and season with salt and pepper. Cover with clingfilm and set aside for at least 1 hour.

Heat a ridged stove-top grill pan over medium heat for 10 minutes until very hot. Arrange the radicchio diagonally across the pan. Turn the pieces with tongs from time to time until striped with grill marks on all sides. Transfer to a serving plate, drizzle with olive oil and serve.

Pannacotta, literally 'cooked cream', comes from Italy and in its classic form is flavoured with vanilla. Italian Galliano, the key ingredient in a Harvey Wallbanger cocktail, is a golden, vanilla-flavoured liqueur. The creamy just-set texture of the pannacotta with summer fruits makes a pleasing change from the usual cream or custard.

pannacotta galliano
with summer fruit compote

200 ml double cream

200 ml milk

2 tablespoons boiling water

75 g caster sugar

2 tablespoons Galliano liqueur or 1 teaspoon
    vanilla essence

1 tablespoon powdered gelatine

summer fruit compote

150 g blueberries (optional)

50–75 g caster sugar

100 g raspberries or loganberries

100 g small strawberries

4 ramekins

serves 4

Put the cream and milk in a small saucepan, simmer gently for 5 minutes over low heat, then add the sugar and the Galliano.

Pour the boiling water into a small heatproof dish and sprinkle the gelatine over the surface (make sure that the tablespoon is level). Leave to stand for a few seconds until the gelatine absorbs the water. Stir until the gelatine has dissolved, then add it to the cream mixture, stirring well. Pour the cream mixture through a sieve into a jug, pushing any bits through the sieve with the back of a wooden spoon. Pour the mixture into 4 ramekins and chill overnight or until set.

To make the summer fruit compote, put the blueberries in a saucepan, if using, with 50 g of the sugar and 2 tablespoons of water. Set over low heat and cook until the juices start to run. Add the raspberries and strawberries, stir carefully, switch off the heat and leave to cool. Taste and add extra sugar, if necessary, then cover and chill until required.

When ready to serve, dip the ramekins of pannacotta quickly in shallow boiling water, then invert onto 4 serving plates. Holding the plate and ramekin together, give it a firm shake, then turn out the pannacotta carefully onto each plate. It should be quite wobbly and will plop out of the ramekin onto the plate. Add a spoonful of compote, then serve.

Variation Serve the pannacotta with shavings of dark chocolate instead of fruit.

nectarines in Sambuca and lime juice

Sambuca is a sweet Italian liqueur made from elderflowers popularized when Italian restaurants took to serving it with a burning coffee bean floating on the top. Its flowery makeup is suited to summer fruits and, if you are lucky enough to live in an area where elder grows, you can strew the delicate little summer flowers over the fruit just before serving.

8 ripe nectarines
3 tablespoons caster sugar
2 tablespoons Sambuca
finely grated zest and freshly squeezed
    juice of 1 unwaxed lime
lime wedges, to serve

serves 4

Slice the nectarines thinly, discarding the stone and put in a bowl. Add the sugar, Sambuca and lime juice, cover and leave for a couple of hours to marinate, if possible. When ready to serve, transfer to serving bowls, then sprinkle with the lime zest and serve with lime wedges.

pineapple, mango, avocado and banana
with white rum and mint

Avocados tend to be served in savoury salads and starters, but in fact their creamy texture and delicate flavour is delicious in fruit salads too. This tropical combination with white rum and mint creates a refreshing and eye-catching close to an *al fresco* summer meal.

1 pineapple, peeled, cored and cut into cubes
1 mango, peeled, stoned and cut into cubes
a handful of fresh mint leaves, plus extra sprigs
    to serve
2 tablespoons white rum
50 g sugar
1 banana
1 avocado

serves 4

Put the pineapple and mango in a bowl, add the mint, rum and sugar and mix well, then cover and chill until required.

When ready to serve, peel and slice the banana, and peel, stone and cut the avocado into cubes. Add to the pineapple and mango and stir well. Serve topped with mint sprigs.

Note If you like, you can serve the fruit in the pineapple shell. Choose a pineapple with fresh green leaves and quarter it lengthways. Take care not to puncture the shell when you remove the flesh, then wrap the pineapple shells in clingfilm and put in the refrigerator until ready to serve.

Frangipane tart is one of those classic recipes that turn a seasonal summer fruit into a luxurious treat. The combination of crisp short pastry, fluffy almond sponge cake and the tart flavours of summer fruits is a delight. Although it is not difficult to make, it does need time devoted to it, but the end result is well worth the effort.

blueberry frangipane tart

To make the pastry, put the ingredients in a bowl and work them quickly and lightly into a smooth ball with your hands. Wrap in clingfilm and chill in the refrigerator for 1 hour.

To make the frangipane, put the sugar and butter in a bowl and beat until light and creamy. Add the eggs a little at a time, beating well as you do so. Add the cornflour, baking powder and almonds, then gently fold into the mixture.

Sprinkle a clean work surface and rolling pin with plenty of flour. Set the pastry in the centre of the flour, then flatten it with the palm of your hand and shape it into a neat circle. Take the rolling pin and roll the pastry one way, then give it a quarter turn and roll it the other way, shaping the dough back into a circle with your hands from time to time. Continue until the pastry is slighty larger than the tin. Roll the pastry loosely around the rolling pin and transfer it carefully to the greased tin, pressing the pastry carefully into the sides. Trim any overlapping pastry and prick the base with a fork.

Add the blueberries, sprinkle with the sugar, then spoon the frangipane over the top, taking care to seal the fruit completely underneath.

Bake in a preheated oven at 180ºC (350ºF) Gas 4 for 45 minutes or until the frangipane is well risen, golden and springy to the touch. After 25 minutes, open the oven door carefully so as not to allow too much heat to escape and, if the tart is getting too brown, lower the heat to 160°C (325°F) Gas 3 for the final 20 minutes. Serve hot or cold dusted with icing sugar.

Variation Try using apricots, peaches, rhubarb or plums, depending on the season.

150 g blueberries, plums or rhubarb
25 g sugar
icing sugar, to serve

pastry
100 g plain flour
10 g cornflour
30 g icing sugar
a pinch of salt
60 g butter, softened
1 small egg yolk
1 tablespoon dry vermouth or iced water

frangipane
100 g caster sugar
100 g butter, softened
2 eggs, lightly beaten
2 tablespoons cornflour
2 teaspoons baking powder
100 g ground almonds

a loose-bottomed tart tin or a pie dish, 20–22 cm diameter, greased

serves 6

Tiramisù is Italian for pick-me-up and this recipe is my summer adaptation of the popular Italian dessert of that name. The original – created in Treviso in the Veneto more years ago than I care to remember – is flavoured with espresso coffee, but it lends itself very well to other flavours, especially fruit, and I have developed several versions according to season.

rhubarb pick-me-up

Put the rhubarb in a saucepan with 100 ml water. Bring to the boil, then add 100 g of the sugar and simmer for about 10 minutes until soft.

Put the rhubarb in a dish and add the aniseed. Stir well, then drain thoroughly and reserve the juice in a large, shallow container.

Put the egg yolks and the remaining sugar in a large bowl and whisk until thick and creamy. Fold in the mascarpone and the grappa, then beat again until smooth.

Put the egg whites in a bowl, whisk until stiff, then fold into the mascarpone mixture.

Make a layer of sponge fingers in a glass dish, dipping each one in the rhubarb juice as you do so. Cover the sponge fingers with half of the rhubarb, then half the mascarpone mixture. Make another layer of sponge fingers and cover with the remaining rhubarb and mascarpone. Cover and refrigerate overnight.

When ready to serve, sprinkle with icing sugar and a little aniseed and decorate with a few whole star anise pods.

Variation Use stewed plums or blueberries instead of rhubarb.

500 g rhubarb, chopped
125 g caster sugar
½ teaspoon ground aniseed,
    plus extra to serve
6 large egg yolks
250 g mascarpone cheese
1 tablespoon grappa or other
    white liqueur
2 egg whites
24 sponge fingers

to serve
icing sugar
3 whole star anise pods

serves 8

drinks

Think of summer and think of long, cooling, colourful drinks enjoyed in the sun. Start the day with a Strawberry and Yoghurt Wake-up Call or a Florida Refresher, go into the afternoon with a Sparkling Iced Mint Tea, then wind down after a long hot day on a Summer Breeze. This chapter is full of traditional and original drinks for every occasion, from old-fashioned homemade cordials, like Lemon Sherbet, to sophisticated cocktails, such as a Bloody Venetian.

131

florida refresher

Citrus fruits are full of vitamin C, as well as being thirst quenching and invigorating. Bars all over Italy have always been geared up to serve freshly squeezed citrus fruit juices, known as *spremute*. No packaged fruit juice, however good, can compare with freshly squeezed fruit juice. This particular combination of juices and kiwi fruit is sensational.

freshly squeezed juice of 2 grapefruit
freshly squeezed juice of 4 oranges
freshly squeezed juice of 2 limes or lemons

to serve
ice cubes
1 kiwi fruit, peeled and sliced
sparkling or still mineral water (optional)
caster sugar

serves 4

Put the fruit juices in a jug, mix well, cover and chill until required. Serve poured over ice cubes in tall glasses and topped with a slice of kiwi. Serve with mineral water and sugar for people to add according to taste.

Variation For a weekend brunch treat, add a measure of white rum, gin or vodka.

al fresco fruit smoothie

Fresh fruit smoothies can be made with any combination of fruit and, needless to say, berryfruits like blackcurrants and raspberries add a lovely colour. Try experimenting with different herbs, such as rosemary, thyme or lavender flowers. You could also try pouring a smoothie over ice cream for a cooling afternoon reviver or a simple dessert, or add lemonade for an old-fashioned ice cream soda.

400 g strawberries
400 g raspberries
400 g melon flesh
4 ice cubes

to serve
4 sprigs of mint or sweet cicely
caster sugar

serves 4

Put the fruit and the ice cubes in a blender and reduce to a purée. Pour into tall glasses and top with sprigs of mint. Serve with sugar for people to add according to taste.

Variation Try other fruits in season, such as combinations of peach, raspberry and apple; or pear, banana and kiwi fruit.

strawberry and yoghurt wake-up call

There are many types of natural yoghurt, ranging from low-fat yoghurt to deliciously rich Greek yoghurt, which, sweetened with honey, is breakfast heaven. My favourite has always been natural set yoghurt, as its mild, sweet, creamy taste is so good on its own. This energizing recipe can be adapted to suit your tastes as blending yoghurt will reduce it to a liquid in any case. If you want to keep it thick, blend the fruit and stir it into the yoghurt.

150 g strawberries, plus 4 small strawberries, to serve
1 large banana, about 150 g, peeled
freshly squeezed juice of ½ lemon
500 ml natural set or Greek yoghurt

to serve
ice cubes
mint sprigs
caster sugar (optional)
muesli (optional)

serves 4

Put the strawberries, banana, lemon juice and yoghurt in a blender and reduce to a purée. Pour into tumblers, add ice cubes and top with mint sprigs. Cut up into the middle of the four remaining strawberries and 'hang' one on each glass. Serve with sugar and muesli, if liked, for people to stir in according to taste.

Variation For a weekend brunch treat, add 4 teaspoons of Cointreau.

lemon sherbet

Old cookery books are full of soft drink recipes, but the advent of manufactured cordials and fizzy drinks has put pay to all that. The high sugar and chemical content of most manufactured soft drinks means that they have little flavour and are not thirst quenching at all. In contrast, this simple recipe for old-fashioned lemonade tastes gorgeous and is totally revitalizing.

thinly pared zest and freshly squeezed juice of
   4 unwaxed lemons
90 g sugar cubes
1 litre boiling water

to serve
1 lemon, sliced
8 ice cubes

makes 1 litre

Wrap half the lemon zest in clingfilm and reserve for later use. Put the remaining zest and the lemon juice in a large heatproof jug with the sugar cubes. Add the boiling water and stir, then cover and leave to cool. Strain and refrigerate. Serve in tall glasses with the lemon slices, a few strips of the reserved lemon zest and ice cubes.

Variation Serve in glasses poured over 2 tablespoons of chopped summer fruit.

sparkling iced mint tea

Cold teas are thirst quenching, stimulating and delicious. Although I use regular tea bags, you could try Earl Grey or other specialist, fruit or herbal teas. The addition of effervescent liquids turns an afternoon classic into a non-alcoholic party drink, making a welcome change from the usual orange juice and lemonade.

2 tea bags or 2 teaspoons leaf tea
500 ml boiling water
125 g sugar
freshly squeezed juice of 3–4 limes
500 ml soda water, tonic water or lemonade
4–6 sprigs of mint, plus extra to serve

to serve
1 lime, sliced
8 ice cubes

makes 1 litre

Put the tea bags in a warmed teapot or heatproof jug with a lid and add the boiling water and the sugar. Stir and leave to stand for 10 minutes. Strain into a heatproof jug and leave to cool. Add the lime juice, cover and chill until required.

Transfer to a large glass jug and add the soda water and mint sprigs. Serve in tall glasses with a slice of lime hooked over the rim with ice cubes and a sprig of mint in each glass.

Variations Use lemon juice instead of lime juice, or add a measure of rum to make an evening drink.

melon and ginger refresher

Root ginger is often associated with warming winter drinks, but it also makes a good summer drink ingredient. It is particularly good in non-alcoholic fruit punches, giving them a tangy kick. To crush ice, place the ice cubes in the middle of a clean tea towel. Enclose the ice in the towel, grasp it tightly and whack it against the work surface until the ice is crushed.

150 g fresh root ginger shavings
thinly pared zest and freshly squeezed juice of
   2 unwaxed lemons
500 g demerara sugar

to serve
1 small melon, peeled, deseeded and diced
crushed ice
sparkling mineral water or soda water

makes 1 litre

Put the ginger and lemon zest in a saucepan, add 500 ml of water and bring to the boil, then reduce the heat and simmer for 30 minutes. Add the sugar and stir well until dissolved, then add the lemon juice and strain into a heatproof jug. Leave to cool, then transfer to screw-top bottles, seal and store in the refrigerator or freezer.

Pour a little of the cordial into a tall glass, add 2 tablespoons of diced melon, fill the glass with crushed ice and top with mineral water. Stir well and serve.

Variation Add a measure of rum.

trafalgar claret cup

This claret cup packs the kind of punch you cannot ignore and should be sipped not slurped. I would not usually recommend drinking punch with food, but this one retains the roundness of a good glass of red wine and it is not overly sweet, even when made with lemonade. Given its strength, a full Nelson was suggested as a suitable name, but since this year is the bicentenary of the battle, I thought Trafalgar a more fitting name.

50 g caster sugar
1 tablespoon boiling water
250 ml brandy
freshly squeezed juice of 1 lemon
leaves from 6 sprigs of mint, plus extra to serve
4 long strips of cucumber peel
750 ml claret
24 ice cubes
750 ml chilled soda water or lemonade

to serve
12 small bunches of red grapes, about 3 grapes in
    each bunch

serves 12

Put the sugar and water in a heatproof bowl and leave until the sugar has dissolved and the mixture has cooled.

Put the sugar solution into a punch bowl or a large jug, add the brandy, lemon juice, mint leaves, cucumber peel and claret, cover and leave to stand for 1–2 hours. When ready to serve, add the ice, stir well and taste. Add soda water to taste. Serve in wine glasses poured over the grapes, topped with mint sprigs.

Variation Add the juice of 1 orange and serve with slices of orange and lemon instead of grapes.

summer breeze

Marinating the strawberries and raspberries in the rum makes for a deliciously fruity drink with a scent of strawberry. The raspberries bleed into the liquid, giving it a pretty shade of pink. Eat the strawberries in your glass halfway down and the flavour changes. This may all sound very light and summery but, mark my words, it's serious stuff.

4 large strawberries, quartered
16 raspberries
40 g caster sugar
250 ml white rum
16 ice cubes
750 ml chilled dry white wine
a dash of chilled lemonade (optional)

serves 8

Put the strawberries and raspberries in a punch bowl or jug, add the sugar and rum and stir well. Cover and leave to stand for at least 1 hour.

When ready to serve, add 8 of the ice cubes, the wine and lemonade, if using. Put an ice cube and a couple of the raspberries and strawberry pieces in each glass, then pour the fruit cup on top.

john's jug o' pimms

Pimm's is the epitome of English outdoor events in the summer. It comes ready-mixed in a bottle and all you need to do is add lemonade and lots of ice. There are, however, certain essential additions, over and above the fruit, namely cucumber and mint. In days gone by, the fruit was served strung onto cocktail sticks with the Pimm's poured over it as suggested in the recipe.

8 slices of red apple, such as gala
8 strawberries or cocktail cherries, sliced
8 slices of lemon or orange
8 slices of cucumber
8 sprigs of mint
750 cl chilled lemonade
250 cl Pimm's No 1
ice cubes, to serve

4 cocktail sticks

serves 4

Put half of the apple, strawberries, lemon and cucumber in a large jug, then add 4 mint sprigs. Add the Pimm's No 1, cover and leave for 1 hour.

Thread the remaining slices of fruit and cucumber onto cocktail sticks. When ready to serve, add the lemonade and stir well. Add a mint sprig and ice cubes to each of 4 goblets or tumblers. Fill with Pimm's No 1 and top with the fruit sticks.

bloody venetian

There are so many cocktails that it is almost impossible to create a new one. This is a marriage of two classics, champagne and mimosa cocktails. My own twist is the use of Prosecco wine and blood red orange juice. Prosecco is a sparkling wine made in the Veneto and sold by the glass in bars and restaurants all over Venice; hence the name Bloody Venetian.

2 tablespoons caster sugar
freshly squeezed juice of 1 lemon
750 ml chilled prosecco or sparkling wine
60 ml Cointreau
60 ml brandy
750 ml chilled blood orange juice
12 ice cubes, to serve

serves 12

Firstly, prepare the glasses. Put the sugar on a plate and spread it out evenly. Wet the rim of a champagne cup or a cocktail glass with lemon juice and dip it into the sugar, twisting the glass as you do so to get a good covering. Repeat with the other glasses.

When ready to serve, pour the Cointreau, brandy and orange juice into a cocktail shaker and shake well. Alternatively, pour the ingredients into a punch bowl and stir well.

Place a few ice cubes in each of 12 glasses, then pour or ladle the cocktail carefully into the glasses, taking care not to wet the sugar crust. Divide the prosecco between the glasses and serve immediately.

virginia mint julep

This recipe comes from an old American cookbook, *The Williamsburg Art of Cookery or Accomplished Gentlewoman's Companion* of 1742. This is the advice printed with it: 'Two Things will inevitably ruin any Julep, the first of which is too much Sugar, and the second is too little Whiskey'. Heeding the warning, I have reduced the original quantity of sugar from 6 to 4 tablespoons. The original recipe called for whiskey made from corn, if you can source it, but your favourite whiskey will do.

5 sprigs of mint
4 tablespoons caster sugar
crushed ice (page 135)
whiskey distilled from corn, such as Kentucky Straight
    Corn Whiskey

serves 4

Divide the leaves from 1 sprig of mint between 4 tall glasses. Add 1 tablespoon of the sugar to each glass and crush together well using a swizzle stick. Add 1 tablespoon of water to each glass to dissolve. Fill the glasses with crushed ice and add as much whiskey as the ice will take. Stir well until the glasses are frosted on the outside, taking care not to wet the outside of the glass. Decorate each glass with the remaining mint sprigs and serve.

bellini

The Bellini was invented in Harry's Bar in Venice and has become popular throughout the Veneto region of Italy. I first came across Bellinis on a hot August night at the romantic Villa Cipriani Hotel in Asolo in the Veneto hills. No Bellini ever tasted better, but then Italian barmen do have a special way with cocktails.

3 white peaches, peeled and stoned
750 ml well-chilled Prosecco

Put the peaches in a food processor and blend to a purée. Transfer to a jug, cover and chill in the refrigerator overnight or until quite cold.

Divide the peach purée between 6 champagne flutes. Add the Prosecco carefully, then stir and serve immediately.

serves 6

index

a

aioli, 50
al fresco dining, 11, 99–129
al fresco fruit smoothie, 132
almonds: blueberry frangipane
    tart, 126
    risotto with Sicilian pesto, 118
anchovies: avocado, olive and
    anchovy dip, 85
    bagna cauda dressing, 40
    bruschetta with crushed butter
    beans and lemon dressing, 45
    herbed lentil salad with hard-
    boiled eggs and, 86
    parsley and anchovy relish, 15
apple tart, traditional English, 97
asparagus, bruschetta with
    pancetta, poached egg and, 46
aubergines: aubergine and tahini
    dip, 85
    caramelized vegetable tarte
    tatin, 60
    grilled aubergine with tahini
    spread, 18
avocados: avocado, olive and
    anchovy dip, 85

    herbed black bean and avocado
    salad, 53
    pineapple, mango, avocado and
    banana, 125

b

bacon: chicken liver, mushroom and
    bacon crostini, 49
bagna cauda dressing, 40
balsamic dressing, 35
barbecues, 9, 13–41
béchamel sauce, 54
beef: fanned steak with rocket crème
    fraîche, 117
    marinated herbed steak served
    panino style, 32
    Nick's barbecued rare roast
    beef, 30–1
beetroot salad, 16
Bellini, 141
black bean and avocado salad, 53
bloody Venetian, 140
blueberry frangipane tart, 126
bread: breadcrumbs, 54
    bruschetta, 45–6
    ciabatta bread filled with roasted

    peppers, Jerusalem hoummus
    and rocket, 82
crostini, 49
hot crusty loaf filled with
    mozzarella, salami and
    tomato, 78
roast pepper, mozzarella and
    Italian cured meat focaccia
    pie, 81
rustic loaf filled with ham and
    apple chutney, 82
bruschetta: asparagus, pancetta and
    poached egg, 46
    baby mozzarella, cherry tomatoes
    and rocket, 45
    crushed butter beans and lemon
    dressing, 45
burger, aromatic pork, 24
butter beans: bruschetta with
    crushed butter beans and
    lemon dressing, 45

c

cake, pineapple and thyme loaf, 93
caramel: caramelized vegetable tarte
    tatin, 60

    fruit platter with spiced caramel,
    63
carpaccio of melon with raspberry
    sauce, 63
Catalan salad with tuna and aioli, 50
charcoal barbecues, 9
cheese: bruschetta with baby
    mozzarella, cherry tomatoes
    and rocket, 45
    cream cheese, walnut and celery
    dip, 85
    hot crusty loaf filled with
    mozzarella, salami and
    tomato, 78
    instant savoury croissants, 69
    penne with mascarpone, spinach
    and pancetta, 56
    roast pepper, mozzarella and
    Italian cured meat focaccia
    pie, 81
    salmon, mascarpone, caper and
    sun-dried tomato crumble, 108
cherry tomato tabbouleh salad, 90
chicken: char-grilled chicken breast
    with mixed leaves and balsamic
    dressing, 35

chicken, ham and mushroom
pies, 59
spiced chicken and mango
mayonnaise, 89
spiced chicken with pistachios
and caramelized peaches, 112
chicken liver, mushroom and bacon
crostini, 49
chickpeas: chickpea and sun-dried
tomato crostini, 49
Jerusalem hoummus with toasted
pine nuts, 85
children's picnics, 10
chillies: chilli tomato chutney, 15
spiked tiger prawns with lime and
chilli marinade, 36
chocolate: triple chocolate chip
muffins, 94
chutney, chilli tomato, 15
ciabatta bread filled with roasted
peppers, Jerusalem hoummus
and rocket, 82
claret cup, Trafalgar, 136
corn-on-the-cob: vegetable
kebabs with bagna
cauda dressing, 40
courgettes: primavera tart, 74
crab: trio of stuffed vegetables, 100
crayfish: speck and crayfish cichetti
laced with chilli, 104
cream: pannacotta Galliano, 122
cream cheese, walnut and celery
dip, 85
croissants, instant savoury, 69
crostini: chicken liver, mushroom and
bacon, 49
chickpea and sun-dried
tomato, 49
crumble, salmon, mascarpone,
caper and sun-dried
tomato, 108
custard: fruit fool, 64

d
dips: aubergine and tahini, 85
avocado, olive and anchovy, 85
cream cheese, walnut and celery,
85
dressings: bagna cauda, 40
balsamic, 35
lemon, 45
yoghurt, 24
drinks: 131–41

e
eggs: bruschetta with asparagus,
pancetta and poached
egg, 46
herbed lentil salad with hard-
boiled eggs and anchovies, 86
electric barbecues, 9
equipment: barbecues, 9

f
fanned steak with rocket crème
fraîche, 117
fennel: caramelized vegetable tarte
tatin, 60
fennel and orange salad, 16
Florida refresher, 132
focaccia pie, 81
foil-wrapped trout with Parma ham,
olives and mushrooms, 39
fool, fruit, 64
frangipane tart, blueberry, 126
French beans with tomato and
garlic, 121
fruit: al fresco fruit smoothie, 132
Florida refresher, 132
fruit fool, 64
fruit platter with spiced caramel,
63
John's jug o' Pimms, 139
pannacotta Galliano with summer
fruit compote, 122

g
gammon: rustic loaf filled with ham
and apple chutney, 82
garlic: aioli, 50
bagna cauda dressing, 40
Sicilian-style lamb cutlets
with lemon and garlic
marinade, 28
gas barbecues, 9
ginger: melon and ginger
refresher, 135
Grannie's scones with whipped
cream and strawberries, 70
grapefruit: Florida refresher, 132
guinea fowl, Italian roast, 114

h
ham: chicken, ham and mushroom
pies, 59
foil-wrapped trout with
Parma ham, olives and
mushrooms, 39
instant savoury croissants, 69
rustic loaf filled with apple chutney
and, 82
speck and crayfish cichetti laced
with chilli, 104
hoummus: ciabatta bread filled with
roasted peppers, Jerusalem
hoummus and rocket, 82
Jerusalem hoummus with toasted
pine nuts, 85
marinated herbed steak served
panino style with tomato, basil
and, 32

i
Italian roast guinea fowl, 114

j
Japanese teriyaki-style spareribs, 27
Jerusalem hoummus with toasted
pine nuts, 85
John's jug o' Pimms, 139

k
kebabs: spiked monkfish, scallops
and cherry tomatoes, 107
vegetable kebabs with bagna
cauda dressing, 40
kiwi, mango and coriander salsa, 15

l
lamb cutlets Sicilian-style with lemon
and garlic marinade, 28
lemon: bruschetta with crushed
butter beans and lemon
dressing, 45
lemon sherbet, 135
Sicilian-style lamb cutlets with
lemon and garlic marinade, 28
lemonade: John's jug o' Pimms, 139
lentils: herbed lentil salad with hard-
boiled eggs and anchovies, 86
lighting barbecues, 9
lime and chilli marinade, spiked tiger
prawns with, 36
liver see chicken liver

m
mangoes: mango, kiwi and coriander
salsa, 15
pineapple, mango, avocado and
banana, 125
spiced chicken and mango
mayonnaise, 89
marinades: lemon and garlic, 28
lime and chilli, 36
teriyaki, 27
mascarpone: rhubarb pick-me-up,
129
salmon, mascarpone, caper and
sun-dried tomato crumble, 108
mayonnaise: aioli, 50
spiced chicken and mango
mayonnaise, 89
melon: carpaccio of melon with
raspberry sauce, 63
melon and ginger refresher, 135
mint: sparkling iced mint tea, 135
Virginia mint julep, 141
monkfish: spiked monkfish, scallops
and cherry tomatoes, 107
muffins, triple chocolate chip, 94
mushrooms: chicken, ham and
mushroom pies, 59
chicken liver, mushroom and
bacon crostini, 49
foil-wrapped trout with Parma
ham, olives and, 39
trio of stuffed vegetables, 100

vegetable kebabs with bagna
cauda dressing, 40

n
nectarines in Sambuca and lime
juice, 124
Nick's barbecued rare roast beef,
30–1
noodles: grilled Thai pork with
stir-fried noodles, 23

o
oranges: fennel and orange
salad, 16
Florida refresher, 132

p
pancakes, Scotch, 67
pancetta: bruschetta with
asparagus, poached egg
and, 46
bruschetta with crushed butter
beans and lemon dressing, 45
penne with mascarpone, spinach
and, 56
panini: marinated herbed steak
served panino style, 32
pannacotta Galliano, 122
Parma ham: foil-wrapped trout with
olives, mushrooms and, 39
instant savoury croissants, 69
parsley and anchovy relish, 15
pasta: instant seafood
spaghetti, 111
penne with mascarpone, spinach
and pancetta, 56
pot luck summer pasta, 54
peaches: Bellini, 141
spiced chicken with pistachios
and caramelized peaches, 112
penne with mascarpone, spinach
and pancetta, 56
peppers: caramelized vegetable tarte
tatin, 60
ciabatta bread filled with roasted
peppers, Jerusalem hoummus
and rocket, 82
grilled peppers with balsamic and
coriander dressing, 19
peperonata, 15
Riviera salad, 16
roast pepper, mozzarella and
Italian cured meat focaccia
pie, 81
trio of stuffed vegetables, 100
vegetable kebabs with bagna
cauda dressing, 40
pesto: risotto with Sicilian pesto, 118
picnics, 10, 73–97
pies: chicken, ham and mushroom
pies, 59
layered salmon, prawn and potato

filo pie, 77
roast pepper, mozzarella and
Italian cured meat focaccia
pie, 81
Pimm's, John's jug o', 139
pineapple: pineapple and thyme loaf
cake, 93
pineapple, mango, avocado and
banana, 125
pork: aromatic pork burger in pita
bread, 24
grilled Thai pork with stir-fried
noodles, 23
Japanese teriyaki-style spareribs,
27
pot luck summer pasta, 54
potatoes: Italian roast guinea fowl
with new potatoes and green
beans, 114
layered salmon, prawn and potato
filo pie, 77
lemon roast potato wedges, 121
new potato, smoked turkey and
chive salad, 53
prawns: layered salmon, prawn and
potato filo pie, 77
spiked tiger prawns with lime and
chilli marinade, 36
primavera tart, 74

r
radicchio plumes, 121
raspberry sauce, carpaccio of melon
with, 63
relish, parsley and anchovy, 15
rhubarb: fruit fool, 64
rhubarb pick-me-up, 129
risotto with Sicilian pesto, 118
Riviera salad, 16
rocket: bruschetta with baby
mozzarella, cherry tomatoes
and, 45
chilled spinach, rocket and
watercress soup, 103
fanned steak with rocket crème
fraîche, 117
rum: summer breeze, 137
rustic loaf filled with ham and apple
chutney, 82

s
safety, barbecues, 9
salads: beetroot salad, 16
Catalan salad with tuna and
aioli, 50
cherry tomato tabbouleh salad, 90
fennel and orange salad, 16
herbed black bean and avocado
salad, 53
herbed lentil salad with hard-
boiled eggs and anchovies, 86

new potato, smoked turkey and
chive salad, 53
Riviera salad, 16
salami, hot crusty loaf filled with
mozzarella, tomato and, 78
salmon: layered salmon, prawn and
potato filo pie, 77
salmon, mascarpone, caper and
sun-dried tomato crumble, 108
sauce, béchamel, 54
scallops: spiked monkfish, scallops
and cherry tomatoes, 107
scones: Grannie's scones with
whipped cream and
strawberries, 70
Scotch pancakes with butter and
caster sugar, 67
seafood spaghetti, instant, 111
sesame sweet potato packets, 20
Sicilian pesto, risotto with, 118
Sicilian-style lamb cutlets, 28
smoothie, al fresco fruit, 132
soup, chilled spinach, rocket and
watercress, 103
soy sauce: teriyaki marinade, 27
spaghetti, instant seafood, 111
spareribs, Japanese teriyaki-style, 27
sparkling iced mint tea, 135
speck and crayfish cichetti laced
with chilli, 104
spiked monkfish, scallops and cherry
tomatoes, 107
spiked tiger prawns with lime and
chilli marinade, 36
spinach: chilled spinach, rocket and
watercress soup, 103
penne with mascarpone, pancetta
and, 56
strawberries: Grannie's scones with
whipped cream and, 70
strawberry and yoghurt wake-up
call, 132
summer breeze, 137
sweet potatoes: sesame sweet
potato packets, 20
sweetcorn: herbed black bean and
avocado salad, 53

t
tabbouleh salad, cherry tomato, 90
tahini: aubergine and tahini dip, 85
grilled aubergine with tahini
spread, 18
tarts: blueberry frangipane tart, 126
caramelized vegetable tarte tatin,
60
primavera tart, 74
traditional English apple tart, 97
tea, sparkling iced mint, 135
teriyaki marinade, 27
Thai pork with stir-fried noodles, 23

tiger prawns with lime and chilli
marinade, 36
tiramisù, 129
tomatoes: bruschetta with baby
mozzarella, cherry tomatoes
and rocket, 45
cherry tomato tabbouleh salad, 90
chickpea and sun-dried tomato
crostini, 49
chilli tomato chutney, 15
hot crusty loaf filled with
mozzarella, salami and, 78
instant seafood spaghetti, 111
layered salmon, prawn and potato
filo pie, 77
marinated herbed steak served
panino style with hoummus,
basil and, 32
peperonata, 15
pot luck summer pasta, 54
primavera tart, 74
risotto with Sicilian pesto, 118
Riviera salad, 16
spiked monkfish, scallops and
cherry tomatoes, 107
Trafalgar claret cup, 136
trio of stuffed vegetables, 100
triple chocolate chip muffins, 94
trout, foil-wrapped with Parma ham,
olives and mushrooms, 39
tuna: Catalan salad with aioli and, 50
pot luck summer pasta, 54
turkey: new potato, smoked turkey
and chive salad, 53

v
vegetables: trio of stuffed
vegetables, 100
vegetable kebabs with bagna
cauda dressing, 40
vinegar: balsamic dressing, 35
Virginia mint julep, 141

w
walnuts: cream cheese, walnut and
celery dip, 85
watercress: chilled spinach, rocket
and watercress soup, 103
whiskey: Virginia mint julep, 141
wine: Bellini, 141
bloody Venetian, 140
summer breeze, 137
Trafalgar claret cup, 136
wood barbecues, 9

y
yoghurt: strawberry and yoghurt
wake-up call, 132
yoghurt dressing, 24